ARABIAN OIL

ARABIAN OIL

✺

AMERICA'S STAKE IN THE MIDDLE EAST

✺

RAYMOND F. MIKESELL
AND
HOLLIS B. CHENERY

THE UNIVERSITY OF NORTH CAROLINA PRESS
Chapel Hill

Copyright, 1949, by

THE UNIVERSITY OF NORTH CAROLINA PRESS

Manufactured in the United States of America

VAN REES PRESS • NEW YORK

PJ

TO OUR PARENTS

PREFACE

THIS BOOK is a product of collaboration between a graduate student and a professor at the University of Virginia. The original draft of this study was presented as a Master's thesis in economics by Mr. Chenery, a petroleum engineer who has turned to the study and teaching of economics. The interest of Mr. Mikesell, under whose direction the thesis was written, stems from his wartime experience in the Middle East and his work as a consultant to the United States government on middle eastern affairs. The diverse backgrounds of the authors have indicated a natural division of labor in the subsequent expansion of the material between the technical problems of petroleum and the financial and other broader aspects of the problem. While each has been primarily responsible for his particular field, both writers take responsibility for the general conclusions of the analysis.

The purpose of this study is three-fold. First we have sought to provide a concise account of America's petroleum position in the Middle East in relation to the world's reserves and production of this vital commodity. Secondly, we have endeavored to present the development of the Arabian oil resources by American firms as a case study in United States foreign economic policy with respect to a strategic material. Although we make no pretense of having provided a comprehensive account of the diplomatic actions and policies of the federal government with respect to Middle East oil, sufficient consideration of this aspect of the problem has been given to enable us to deal with our third purpose, namely, to make suggestions for a United States foreign petroleum policy. We have approached this third objective with considerable temerity. Political and economic factors which have a bearing on the determination of an appropriate foreign oil policy are subject to rapid change. Hence our conclusions on this problem should be considered more in the nature of considerations than as representing a definitive program.

This book has been sponsored and its publication financed by the Richmond Area University Center. The authors wish to express their gratitude to the members of the Research Council of the Richmond Area University Center and to its chairman, Dr. E. W. Gregory, Jr., for making it possible to publish this study.

The authors wish to express their sincere appreciation to the Institute for Research in the Social Sciences of the University of Virginia and to its Director, Professor Wilson Gee, for assistance in the preparation of the manuscript and making arrangements for its publication. We are also indebted to the following people for their kindness in reading the manuscript and for making valuable suggestions: Mr. Basil Manly, formerly Chairman of the Federal Power Commission, Mr. John Loftus, Professor of Economics at the Advanced School for International Studies and former Chief of the Petroleum Division in the Department of State, Mr. Robert Eakens of the Department of State, Mr. Phillip Kidd of the Arabian-American Oil Company, Mr. Paul McGuire, Lt. Col. R. H. McCutcheon, and Mr. C. T. Chenery. It should be emphasized that the foregoing are in no way responsible for conclusions or for any of the errors of judgment or fact which may be found in this monograph. Finally we owe a debt of gratitude to Miss Ruth Ritchie, Secretary of the Institute for Research in the Social Sciences, who labored without complaint through successive drafts of the manuscript.

CONTENTS

	Preface	vii
I.	Introduction	1
II.	The World's Petroleum Position	14
III.	The Middle East in World Oil Production	26
IV.	The Concessions and the Companies	37
V.	American Petroleum Development in Bahrein and Saudi Arabia	58
VI.	The Impact of Oil on the Arabian Economy	71
VII.	Middle East Oil and United States Foreign Policy	90
VIII.	Prospects and Conclusions	110
IX.	Some Recent Developments	129
	Appendices	
	1. International Petroleum Economics	145
	2. Statistical Appendix	176
	3. "An Agreement on Petroleum between the Government of the United States of America and the Government of the United Kingdom of Great Britain and Northern Ireland"	185
	"Charter of a Petroleum Reserves Corporation"	190
	"Outline of Proposed Arabian Pipe-line Agreement"	192
	Index	199

TABLES

Estimated Landed Cost in United States of Foreign and Domestic Crude Oil	19
Production and Reserves of the Seven Largest Oil Companies Producing Abroad	21
Production and Reserves in the Middle East	27
Estimated Capital Expenditures in Oil Production, 1948-1953	138
Estimates of Capital Invested by United States Companies	147
Weight of Steel Required for Various Diameters of Pipe	150
Estimated Transport Costs for Various Load Factors: "Big Inch" 24-Inch Crude Oil Line, Texas to New York	150
Cost of Crude Oil Transportation per Ton-Mile	152
Direct Cost of Refining	152
Typical Prewar Refinery Costs in the United States	153
Capital Intensity in United States Petroleum Industry	155
World Oil Reserves and Ownership	177
World Petroleum Balance Sheet, 1946	178
Interregional Movements of Petroleum, 1946	179
United States Supply and Exports of Petroleum	180
Middle East Oil Companies	181
Middle East Oil Production	182
Petroleum Export-Import Forecast, 1955	183
Middle East Pipe Lines	184

ARABIAN OIL

CHAPTER I

INTRODUCTION

CURRENT PUBLIC INTEREST in Arabian oil is greater than in any other single foreign activity of American private enterprise. The spectacular discoveries of a strategic resource in desert countries about which little is known, the diplomatic struggles of the great powers, and the romantic appeal of the Middle East have stirred the imagination of the world. But behind this drama American oil companies are creating what may well become our most important single foreign investment from the standpoint of size and its significance to the American economy.

The story of a foreign investment can no longer be written in terms of profit and loss calculations of private enterprise. In recent years foreign investments have become to an increasing degree matters of national policy. Although this is true of foreign investments in general, governmental interest is especially keen in international ventures which have for their objective the exploitation of a strategic commodity such as petroleum. In discussing American petroleum interests in the Middle East a substantial portion of our analysis will therefore be concerned with the broader economic and political factors which help to determine the policies of the nations concerned. Now that oil has been discovered and reasonably reliable estimates of reserves determined, the key to the future development of petroleum in the Middle East will be found not so much in the profit and loss statements of the private companies but in the international, economic, and political environment of the postwar period. This environment relates to such factors as political relations between the Middle East countries and other powers, governmental policies of the Middle East countries with respect to foreign investment, the pattern of international trade, international business practices and corporate relations, international agreements with respect to the production and sale of petroleum, and the system of international payments.

Before taking up the story of American activities in the Middle East we will set the stage for these complex developments by a brief outline of America's investments in foreign petroleum throughout the world, followed by a discussion of the national interest of the United States in this important resource.

AMERICA'S INTEREST IN FOREIGN PETROLEUM

United States companies have been active in all of the important oil producing areas with the exception of the U.S.S.R. and Iran. They have been responsible for most of the development in such major producing countries as Mexico, Venezuela, Colombia, Rumania, and more recently in Bahrein, Saudi Arabia, and Kuwait. American companies own 40 per cent of the proved crude oil reserves outside of the United States.[1] They currently account for more than one third of foreign production, the greater part of which is marketed abroad through subsidiaries of the producing companies.[2]

The exploitation of foreign oil resources on a large scale by American enterprise did not begin until after World War I. In 1920 it was forecast that United States production would reach a maximum in two to five years and decline thereafter, forcing us to rely increasingly on foreign sources.[3] Our gov-

1. See Appendix II for data on ownership of world's petroleum reserve.
2. In 1944 United States foreign production plus direct United States exports totalled 44 per cent of the world's consumption outside of the United States. See "United States Petroleum Import Prospects," *Industrial Reference Service*, Department of Commerce, July, 1947.
3. As late as 1926 the Federal Oil Conservation Board estimated that our proved reserves were only 4½ billions of barrels, or six years' supply.

ernment strongly encouraged the oil companies to augment their supplies by exploring foreign fields. In 1920 a bill was introduced into the Senate providing for the formation of a United States Oil Corporation, which, had it passed, would have put the government into partnership with the oil industry for the development of oil reserves abroad. Its rejection was in line with our traditional *laissez faire* policy.

Spurred by the threatened domestic shortage and government encouragement, American oil companies, large and small, sent geologists and drillers into most of the countries favorable to oil occurrence. The decade of the twenties saw a great expansion of our foreign drilling concessions, as the emphasis shifted from marketing to production. Most of this exploration activity was in Latin America, where United States corporations now control 65 per cent of the proved reserves. Mexico had the most spectacular development, and American companies were responsible for most of its production until the industry was nationalized by the Mexican government.

After fears of an oil shortage had been dissipated in 1930, many companies withdrew from foreign operations. The coincidence of the reduced demand for petroleum products in the depression years and the discovery of huge reserves in east Texas threatened to demoralize the industry. For the next decade oil companies concentrated chiefly on the domestic problems of oversupply and conservation. The securing of large concessions by American companies in Arabia in 1933 and 1934 went practically unnoticed at the time, and public interest in foreign oil was not renewed until World War II threatened our domestic supplies.

Because large sums of capital are necessary for ventures in foreign oil exploitation, the large companies dominate foreign production to a far greater degree than in the domestic industry. In addition to the considerable risks involved in all petroleum exploitation, tremendous investments in foreign fields are usually required over a considerable period before a barrel of oil is produced or any returns materialize.[4] This time lag is largely due to the protracted negotiations which are necessary for the procurement of foreign concessions and the difficulties of operating in the primitive areas where most of the world's oil occurs. Legal problems are legion. Since in most countries subsoil rights adhere to the sovereign power, negotiations for concessions usually have to be carried on with the governments concerned. These contracts are not always respected by succeeding governments. Where a concession is sought in a dependency of another power, negotiations have to be carried on with both the local government and the controlling power. Because of the nature of its occurrence the search for oil is a speculative business at best, to which is added the risk of political uncertainties.

Petroleum accounts for a larger share of direct United States investments abroad than any other industry. At the beginning of World War II direct investments of American firms in petroleum operations amounted to 18 per cent of our total foreign direct investments.[5] Eleven United States companies have significant foreign investments in petroleum, but 98 per cent of our foreign oil reserves are owned by five companies. These five companies are among the seven largest domestic oil companies and also among the seventeen largest industrial corporations in the United States. The remaining American oil companies which have foreign interests operate almost entirely in South America. American petroleum acquisitions in the Middle East were until 1948 controlled entirely by the five major companies.

From the standpoint of relative production costs, foreign

---

4. Some outstanding examples of individual company investments:
   Colombia: $60,000,000 invested since 1916; no returns until 1939.
   Iraq: $62,000,000 invested since 1925; returns began 1934.
   Venezuela: $44,000,000 invested; returns after 15 years.
   Netherlands East Indies: $39,000,000 invested before returns.
   American Petroleum Interests in Foreign Countries, Hearings, Special Committee Investigating Petroleum Resources, U. S. Senate, 79th Congress, 1st Session, June 27 and 28, 1945, pp. 277 ff.

5. *Petroleum Interests in Foreign Countries*, p. 181.

oil operations have proved very attractive to American companies. In 1945 the capital expenditure required abroad was only 43 cents per barrel of oil produced compared to 78 cents at home.[6] The average cost of finding the oil owned by the United States abroad has been estimated at less than 10 cents per barrel,[7] which is less than one-fifth of the present cost in the United States. Since our exploration and production costs are likely to rise more rapidly than foreign costs in the future, this difference may increase.

American petroleum interests abroad have suffered considerably as a result of World War II and its aftermath. Heavy damage to fields and refineries occurred in the Netherlands East Indies and the countries of Central Europe. Some of these fields have not yet been turned over to their owners. In the case of properties in Rumania, Austria, and Hungary, the Russian-dominated governments have imposed conditions on the owners which make profitable operation impossible.

In a number of instances foreign governments have nationalized their petroleum industries, usually at considerable loss to the American and British companies whose properties were taken over.[8] In other countries the threat of nationalization has led to revision of established contracts to the companies' disadvantage.[9] Nationalization in the consuming countries (notably Europe) has led to the imposition of many restrictions on refiners and marketers. High tariffs on refined products have induced American petroleum companies to build uneconomic refineries in the countries where their products are sold. France and Italy are the chief examples of such

6. J. S. Pogue, *Financial and Operating Data for Thirty Oil Companies*, 1945, p. 18.
7. See "United States Petroleum Import Prospects," p. 9.
8. Examples of alleged losses to Americans through expropriation are: Bolivia (1937): Loss to one company of $15,000,000; Mexico: Loss to four companies of $80,000,000; Russia and Italy: Losses not known. *Petroleum Interests in Foreign Countries*, pp. 245 ff.
9. Compulsory revisions of existing concession contracts in Iran (1933) and Venezuela (1943) are examples of revisions which were probably justified on the basis of the decrease in risk which accompanies fuller development.

practices. Before the war these countries raised the price of petroleum products to the consumer to enable government-controlled distributors to compete more favorably with foreign companies.[10]

QUESTIONS OF NATIONAL INTEREST

An important purpose of this book is to discuss the role of United States foreign policy in the development of American petroleum in the Middle East. Two world wars have focused the attention of Congress, the administration, and the public upon the need for a positive program with respect to overseas oil which would be closely integrated with a program for domestic production. Middle East oil is especially significant in the development of this program for two reasons. First, recent discoveries in the Middle East have indicated that the Middle East fields are likely to achieve a dominant position in the production of petroleum and that the oil center of the world is shifting from the Western to the Eastern Hemisphere. And second, American companies have acquired a major interest in the exploitation of Middle Eastern oil.

In the development of a long-range foreign oil program several important questions of national interest must be kept in mind. First of all there is the matter of giving encouragement, assistance, and protection to American private enterprise operating abroad. This interest is not necessarily an expression of American imperialism but is firmly rooted in the American economic philosophy of free enterprise. It may be defended on economic grounds in terms of the benefits which derive from a free flow of international investment, particularly from countries like the United States with a surplus of investment capital. However, most nations have come to regard investments by foreign enterprises as a matter of special concern of the government so that the foreign activities of American corporations are no longer regarded as a matter of right but as subject to the discretion of the government in which the investment is to be made. This is particularly true

10. *Petroleum Interests in Foreign Countries*, pp. 241-53.

INTRODUCTION 7

in the case of petroleum concessions which involve rights to sub-soil resources usually owned or controlled by the governments themselves.

Since the United States recognizes the right of foreign governments to control the activities of foreign concerns within their borders, our traditional open-door policy can only have meaning in terms of the willingness of foreign governments to permit American concerns to compete for oil concessions on more or less equal terms with the companies of other nationalities. So many factors are involved in the granting of concessions, however, that the principle of competitive bidding and award to the highest bidder is not likely to prove feasible in practice. On several occasions the United States State Department has insisted on the principle of equal access in the granting of concessions in mandates and other dependent areas under the control of a foreign power.

Another aspect of national interest relates to the protection of American firms operating abroad against expropriation, unfair treatment, and burdensome restrictions on production, trade, and foreign exchange transactions. Considerable criticism of the State Department's activities in providing diplomatic protection was expressed by oil company representatives during the hearings before the Special Senate Committee Investigating Petroleum Resources.[11] There are, however, limitations on how far our diplomatic officials can go in extending such protection without our being accused of attempting to interfere with the sovereign rights of other nations. The right of every sovereign nation to control the activities of foreign enterprises operating within its borders is firmly established and this right can be limited only by treaties with other powers. The best way to assure adequate protection for our nationals abroad is through international conventions which set up standards of fair treatment for foreign enterprises. Although our commercial treaties with foreign countries deal with many aspects of this problem, much more

11. See *American Petroleum Interests in Foreign Countries*, pp. 311 ff.

remains to be done.[12] A beginning at least has been made in the *Charter for an International Trade Organization*[13] which states that members of the ITO agree to provide reasonable opportunities for foreign investments on a non-discriminatory basis and adequate security for existing and future investments. These general undertakings, however, need to be strengthened by specific agreements with respect to the taxation of foreign investments, the right to transfer earnings and capital, and other matters of vital concern to foreign investors.

The encouragement and protection of American enterprises operating in foreign fields is closely related to our national interest in securing adequate sources of foreign oil to augment our own production. In a world in which the principle of free access to supplies of raw materials operates in an ideal fashion it would not matter what country's nationals operated the petroleum fields since presumably supplies would be available to all nations on equal terms. But the realization of this principle cannot be relied upon, especially in periods of crisis, so that national interest may dictate that an adequate proportion of the world's supply should be in the hands of firms subject to the jurisdiction of the United States Government.[14]

Once a country has established a profitable foreign concession a number of special economic and political problems immediately emerge, and with respect to these a national policy must be determined. There is inevitably an interest in the nature and stability of the government of the concession country, and a desire to prevent its being influenced by a third power in a manner inimical to the interest of the con-

12. See *Conditions of Private Foreign Investment*, League of Nations publication. (New York: Columbia University Press, 1946).
13. *Havana Charter for the International Trade Organization* (Department of State, 1948), Article 12.
14. Very often, however, the distribution of the raw material is determined by the government of the country in which the resource is produced. For example, oil from British and American-owned wells and refineries is being directed to Russia by the Russian-dominated government of Rumania.

cessionaire. The implementation of these objectives may include economic assistance to the concession country and diplomatic maneuvers of various kinds.

A final question of national interest has to do with our cartel policy. The vast bulk of American foreign petroleum operations is in the hands of a few giant companies frequently allied with one another and with large foreign organizations. This is not merely a matter of how the activities of these combines may affect the degree of competition in domestic markets. It also concerns our international cartel policy as set forth in the *Charter for an International Trade Organization*. Production and marketing agreements between large oil concerns operating over wide areas of the world, such as the famous "Redline Agreement" [15] entered into by the owners of the Iraq Petroleum Company in 1928 and the recent agreements involving the Anglo-Iranian Oil Company and American oil companies operating in the Middle East, have far-reaching international, economic, and political implications. Closely related to this problem is the need for an international understanding among the nations of the world that the world's petroleum resources will be utilized for the benefit of mankind generally and not become a source of rivalry among the Great Powers or a source of hatred and resentment among the smaller powers which lack access to sources of supply.

Turning to the interests of the country in which the investment is made, there are, in addition to the desire for large revenues from royalties and local expenditures for labor and materials, certain broad economic and political considerations which must be reckoned with. Governments are jealous of their sovereignty and are fearful of the establishment of powerful foreign organizations on their soil. In addition they want, or should want, the foreign investment to contribute to a well-rounded development of their economy. Large foreign expenditures and the sudden acquisition of large revenues from royalty payments may create internal strains and

15. For full explanation of this see below, pp. 45 ff.

maladjustments in the economy of a small country. Careful planning and close cooperation between the local government and the foreign concessionaire are necesary to assure that the new source of wealth and business activity will result in the maximum social and economic benefits to the inhabitants.

Finally, there must be considered the national interests of third countries, both as producers and consumers of petroleum. As a competitor for concessions in undeveloped areas, this country has adhered to the principle of equal access or the open door. In effect this principle means that no country should seek by diplomatic or other means to prevent another country from obtaining a concession in third countries or in mandated areas even though the former country has close political ties with the country in which the concession is desired. In practice, however, this does not mean that all countries have equal access to the undiscovered petroleum sources of the world. The cost of developing large concessions, often running into several hundred million dollars, is prohibitive to all but a handful of giant companies owned by the nationals of large industrial countries. Since large markets for petroleum products are frequently thousands of miles from the centers of production, producers must have large marketing organizations, refineries, and transport facilities such as tanker fleets and pipe lines. A few small countries are able to utilize their own petroleum resources for internal use, but for the reasons stated above, active competition for foreign concessions now boils down to competition among four powers, Great Britain, the United States, Russia, and France.

Equally significant from the standpoint of the national interest of third countries is their position as consumers. In the past equal access to raw materials has been interpreted to mean the ability of all countries to purchase the commodities at the same price, with each country being allotted an equitable share in the event of a world shortage. With the development of exchange controls and increasing trade restrictions in recent years this concept of equal access has become altogether too narrow. Companies with foreign concessions have

INTRODUCTION

tended to sell the output of their wells and refineries for their own currencies just as though the petroleum were being produced within their own borders. This creates a foreign exchange problem for other countries whose exports to the countries in control of the supply of petroleum have not increased.[16] It is not enough to permit countries to buy oil for dollars on the same terms as Americans; they must be afforded an opportunity to obtain the dollars as well.

UNITED STATES OIL DIPLOMACY IN THE PAST

Prior to World War II it cannot be said that the United States had a foreign oil policy or program which was separate and distinct from our general international commercial policy. In carrying out our general commercial policy with respect to American firms operating abroad the Department of State gave diplomatic assistance and support to our foreign oil operations along the following general lines: [17]

(1) It sought to prevent discrimination against American firms marketing oil in foreign countries.

(2) It insisted upon the open-door principle of equal commercial opportunity with respect to the granting of concession contracts for the exploration and development of foreign oil.

(3) It asked that American firms be given just and adequate compensation where a foreign government has expropriated American oil properties.

(4) The American Government on various occasions rendered diplomatic assistance to American oil firms in dealing with foreign governments.

All of these activities are routine and have been carried on with respect to American foreign operations in commodities

16. For example petroleum exports to Europe by American concerns operating in Latin America have been sold largely for dollars. American-produced Persian Gulf Oil has also been sold for dollars.

17. For a discussion of American foreign oil policy see John A. Loftus, "Oil in United States Foreign Policy," an address delivered at the University of Pittsburgh on July 30, 1946, and reprinted in the *Oil and Gas Journal*, August 1946.

other than oil. However, there are several instances in which our diplomatic actions have been so vigorous in furthering our interest in the acquisition of foreign oil reserves that they appear to go beyond the normal activities in the enforcement of our general commercial policy. One of these cases involved the participation of American firms in the exploration and development of Mesopotamia (now Iraq), which became a British mandate after World War I. At the conference of San Remo, Britain entered into an agreement with the French Government whereby the oil produced in this area would be shared by the British and the French and that any private company which might develop the Mesopotamian fields "shall be under permanent British control." In 1920 the United States State Department [18] protested vigorously against this action and charged the British with restricting American competition by debarring foreigners and foreign nationals from owning or operating oil-producing properties in the British Isles, colonies, and protectorates. In particular the United States Government protested the British violation of the open-door principle under which League of Nations mandates were to be governed.[19] After several years of negotiation and diplomatic exchanges the British Government retreated from its earlier position with respect to Iraq and admitted American participation. Similar steps were taken by the State Department when Britain sought to interfere with the acquisition of oil concessions by American firms in Bahrein Island and Kuwait, both of which are British protectorates.

Another important controversy occurred when the Netherlands Government tried to keep American concerns from obtaining additional concessions in the Dutch East Indies.

18. See *Diplomatic Protection of American Petroleum Interests in Mesopotamia, Netherlands East Indies, and Mexico*, by H. S. Fraser, Counsel for the Special Senate Committee Investigating Petroleum Resources, Senate Document No. 43, 79th Congress, 1st Session.

19. The British took the position that since the United States was not a signatory of the Versailles Treaty and not a member of the League, it was not entitled to participate in the development of the mandates.

In addition to a formal protest by the State Department, Secretary of the Interior Fall denied the application of the Roxana Petroleum Company, a subsidiary of Royal Dutch Shell, for permission to lease oil lands of the Creek Indians in Oklahoma. This action was later rescinded after the Netherlands Government allotted concessions to the Standard Oil Company of New Jersey in Sumatra and other Dutch East Indies islands.

Domestic discoveries in the late 1920's and early 1930's eliminated the threatened oil shortage, so the United States Government's interest in opening the doors to American participation in foreign oil production waned. Our most important concession, that in Saudi Arabia, was secured early in the 1930's without any assistance from the American Government. It was not until 1939 that our interests in Saudi Arabia were thought sufficiently important to warrant the sending of a diplomatic representative to that country, and an American Legation was not established in Jidda until 1942.

Since 1943 the United States Government has pursued a policy of strong government support to our oil interests abroad. During the war the State Department added a number of petroleum attachés to its embassy staffs, and cooperation between the government and this industry is closer than ever before. In 1944 the United States Government came very near to being a direct participant in foreign oil operations in Arabia. More recently the government has directed its efforts toward the development of an international agreement for the realization of its foreign petroleum objectives. So far these objectives have been variously expressed by congressional and administrative spokesmen, but they have not taken a definite form. Many of the weightiest problems involved in the determination of our international oil policy arise directly out of American penetration in the Middle East.

CHAPTER II

THE WORLD'S PETROLEUM POSITION

An ADEQUATE APPRAISAL of American petroleum operations in the Middle East requires an understanding of the current and prospective petroleum position of the world. Since world markets are closely interrelated and supplied by a few large companies, no producing area can be treated in isolation. We must also give special consideration to the United States, not only as the largest producer and consumer of petroleum, but as the leading power in the international oil trade. Because of this dual role, our domestic requirements have an important bearing on our foreign oil policy. The fact that the rate of foreign oil discovery is increasing much more rapidly than our domestic rate presages a major shift in the pattern of oil production and distribution in the next decade. The extent of this shift will depend in large measure upon the policy decisions of governments as well as the purely economic and technological factors governing the policies and operations of the international oil companies.[1]

WORLD RESERVES AND PRODUCTION

The world's oil reserves are concentrated to a large extent in several geologically favorable regions. The primary requirement is the existence of sedimentary rocks. The most favorable areas are basins where the earth's surface has been sinking slowly and has allowed great thicknesses of sediment to accumulate. While several of these ancient basins exist in northern North America and Central Asia, the great bulk of the world's oil reserves has been found in tropical and sub-tropical regions.

[1]. All statistical data used in this chapter will be found in Appendix II.

The Gulf of Mexico-Caribbean basin and the Persian Gulf-Caspian Sea basin contain at least 80 per cent of the world's discovered oil. They are also the most likely areas for future discoveries.

Until the recent war the United States has always been the world's largest exporter of petroleum products as well as the largest consumer. Since the beginning of the industry in 1860 we have produced some 63 per cent of the world's oil and consumed nearly that much. In recent years our exports of refined products have been increasingly offset by imports of crude from the Caribbean, and the latter area has now become the world's largest exporter of crude oil.

The proved petroleum reserves [2] of the world are presently estimated at over seventy billion barrels. These are distributed among the major regions as follows: Middle East, 45 per cent; United States, 30 per cent; Russia, 8 per cent; Caribbean (chiefly Venezuela), 13 per cent. This concentration of known reserves leaves only 4 per cent to be distributed among the rest of the countries of the world. Although the United States at present has about a third of the world's reserves, it has only about a sixth of the world area favorable to oil occurrence. The limitations of United States reserves are much better known than those of foreign countries, since exploration in the United States has been over one hundred times more intensive. It is therefore highly unlikely that we can keep on producing anything like our present large share of the world's oil from domestic resources.

Because of the relatively recent discovery of the major fields of the Middle East,[3] the present distribution of petroleum production bears little relation to the proved reserves of the pro-

2. "Proved reserves" are based on scientific estimates of the amounts of oil remaining in the ground which have been discovered by actual drilling and are recoverable by existing economical methods. The estimates are subject to constant alteration on the basis of information from new wells, the introduction of new methods, and from price changes.

3. This history of middle eastern production will be detailed in the next chapter.

ducing areas. In the past the rate of development of foreign fields has been determined by nearness to consuming centers and the ease of exploitation rather than the extent of the oil reserves. Until recently, the markets which the Middle East might serve could be supplied more easily from existing wells in the Caribbean and the United States. Even now, production in the Middle East is only 1 per cent of proved reserves, compared to 7 per cent in the Western Hemisphere. In the present transitional period, the Western Hemisphere is bearing more than its share of the burden of supplying the world with oil. The Eastern Hemisphere is a net importer of about a quarter of its total consumption, despite the fact that its reserves are greater than those of the West.

AMERICA'S PETROLEUM BALANCE SHEET

At the close of 1947 exports and imports of petroleum products by the United States were almost exactly balanced, and by mid-1948 there was an import surplus of 100,000 barrels per day. Only a minority of expert opinion sees much likelihood of a continuing increase in the present rate of United States production of petroleum products—5,600,000 barrels per day—while a continued increase in consumption seems inevitable. The alternatives facing the country are either a substantial reliance on imports or the development of other sources of liquid fuel. Both alternatives will be considered.

Although proved reserves in the United States are at an all-time high, their ratio to annual production has been declining since 1938. The present ratio of eleven to one is considerably lower than the "normal" fifteen years supply which the industry should have for efficient operation and conservation. Only once has the reserve ratio fallen lower—during the postwar oil shortage of 1923. The new discoveries of oil in the past five years have been less than the amount produced, even if allowance is made for the normal upward revisions of the initial estimates.[4] While more intensive wildcatting may be

4. *National Resources and Foreign Aid*, Report of Secretary of Interior J. A. Krug, October 9, 1947, p. 81.

able to improve this record somewhat if crude oil prices continue to rise, the chances of discovering large fields decline as more areas are explored.[5] The most optimistic forecast is that United States crude production will increase moderately over the next twenty years. However it is quite possible that production will decline to 3,500,000 barrels per day. On the other hand our domestic peacetime requirements may reach 7 million barrels per day by 1955. A far-sighted program should be prepared for the most pessimistic eventuality.

Aside from an increasing reliance on imports, what sources are available for meeting the increasing deficit of crude petroleum? The answer to this question depends partly upon the price to which crude is allowed to rise. If we are not to rely upon a large quantity of imports, we must accept the probability that domestic crude will be produced at a steadily increasing cost. The cost of finding oil in the United States has risen from $.09 a barrel in 1935-37 to $.45 in 1945.[6] Although exploratory and drilling technique are constantly being improved, they are being more than offset by the increased depth of wells and the smaller discoveries. While this trend is by no means conclusive (1947 additions to reserves were the greatest since 1937) it is a warning that we must consider alternative sources of supply.[7]

Research and developmental work are now under way to determine the feasibility of producing gasoline and other products from a variety of raw materials: natural gas, coal, tar sands, and oil shales. Synthesis of gasoline from natural gas has already begun on a commercial scale. As natural gas is needed

5. The number of exploratory wells necessary to find adequate new reserves has constantly increased. Between 1936 and 1946 the oil discovered per wildcat well drilled declined from 1180 thousand barrels to 160. *Petroleum Data Book*, 1948, p. C-30.

6. *Petroleum Data Book*, 1947, p. C-78. Inflation has of course raised the dollar cost considerably since 1945. More significant is the declining discovery rate per well. Production costs have more than doubled over the same period.

7. The record of oil discovery over the past five years is as good as it was in the decade of 1916-1925. We cannot assume, however, that another east Texas field will be discovered in the years to come.

for other important uses, and it cannot offset the impending oil shortage to any large degree. If gas discoveries continue according to present trends, a maximum of 500,000 barrels per day of oil products could be obtained from synthesis if other demands for gas are to be filled.[8] This would involve the use of 40 per cent of the expected additions to our natural gas reserves for the production of gasoline.

From the standpoint of the abundance of domestic raw materials, production from coal and oil shale is a far more promising alternative. More work needs to be done to make these sources available, but pilot plants are being established by both the government and private industry for this purpose. Reserves of these two raw materials are probably sufficient to meet our demands for liquid fuel for a thousand years. Latest cost estimates indicate that in the most favorable locations they would be only slightly more expensive than crude as a source of gasoline.[9] In comparing the relative advantages of production from shale oil and coal, the latter has certain distinct advantages. First shale oil is found largely in the mountain states and therefore remote from the principal marketing areas. Also coal mining is an established industry which in normal times has a substantial surplus capacity. Finally, the residue from the production of gasoline from coal can be used for the production of commercially marketable by-products, while in the case of the refining of shale oil, the residue is almost entirely waste material.

Before we embrace synthetic fuels as the solution to the impending gasoline shortage in the United States, however, we must consider the investment necessary for an output of the order of magnitude which is contemplated. It is estimated that productive capacity of one million barrels per day of synthetic fuels would require 225 million tons of coal a year,

---

8. E. V. Murphree, President of Standard Oil Development Co. in the *Oil and Gas Journal*, April 8, 1948, p. 66. See also *The Lamp*, March, 1947 for discussion of alternative sources of liquid fuels.

9. See *Reports of Secretary of Interior on the Synthetic Liquid Fuel Act* for 1946 and 1947.

150,000 miners, and 10,000,000 tons of steel.[10] Coal production requires much more labor than does oil for a comparable output, and the amount of equipment needed for the synthetic process is considerably greater than that necessary to refine crude oil. Clearly a large scale synthetic oil project would have serious disadvantages so long as both labor and steel are in short supply. For the long run, the increased cost of perhaps one or two dollars a barrel over imported crude must be weighed against the independence from foreign sources which we would achieve by an investment in synthetic production.

TABLE 1

ESTIMATED LANDED COST PER BARREL ON UNITED STATES EAST COAST OF FOREIGN AND DOMESTIC CRUDE OIL *

	Arabian	Venezuelan	U. S. Gulf Coast
			(1947
Cost of production †	$.30	$.50	$1.85 market
Royalty and taxes	.21	.35 ‡	price)
Transportation §	.75	.20	.35
U. S. import tax	.105	.105	
Difference in refinery realization	.20	.10	
Profit	.25	.25	
Total cost	$1.82	$1.51	$2.20

* Source: *U. S. Petroleum Import Prospects.*

† Maximum estimates; current production costs probably less in both foreign areas.

‡ Estimated, as of 1946.

§ Assuming use of company-owned tankers and completion of Trans-Arabian pipe line. Present U. S. Maritime Commission rate to New York (including Suez Canal toll of 18¢ per barrel) is $1.72 per barrel. By using large tankers currently under construction it is estimated that cost could be reduced to $1.27 a barrel.

Imports are obviously the cheapest way to meet our fuel requirements. The preceding table gives an estimate of the

10. Testimony of W. C. Schroeder, Chief of Office of Synthetic Fuels, Department of Interior, before the Wherry committee. Quoted in the *Oil and Gas Journal,* October 25, 1947, p. 65.

cost of foreign crude landed on the east coast of the United States as compared with the landed cost of Texas crude.

Caribbean crude, including transportation to the east coast, is considerably cheaper than United States crude, while Persian Gulf sources are now competitive and will be substantially cheaper than U.S. Gulf crude as soon as the projected pipe lines to the Mediterranean are completed. However Persian Gulf sources are likely to be largely utilized in supplying the needs of Europe for some time to come.[11]

The trend of discovery and production costs will inevitably favor foreign over domestic sources. The production rate of the average United States well is 11 barrels of crude per day, compared to 220 in Venezuela and 4,000 in the Middle East. Transportation costs are the largest item in the cost of imported oil, but these costs will be reduced by the construction of larger tankers and pipe lines. There is every evidence that the cost of imported oil is likely to remain low for many years to come while domestic costs are almost certain to rise. The foreign reserves controlled by American companies should be able to supply our import requirements for an indefinite period of time should we decide to rely on them.

The choice between increasing imports and increasing subsidies to domestic producers (in the form of tariffs or otherwise) must be made on political as well as economic grounds. If the United States is to take a larger and larger share of Caribbean exports, the Middle East must be developed as rapidly as possible to supply the Eastern Hemisphere. It is quite possible that new developments in the field of oil synthesis will reduce the present cost advantage of imported petroleum. This is still a moot question, but it should be kept in mind in the consideration of our interests in the Middle East.

THE INTERNATIONAL PETROLEUM INDUSTRY

The petroleum industry outside of the United States is divided between state-owned enterprises and a few large

11. See Appendix I for analysis of world demand for petroleum.

American and British companies. Although several Latin American countries have state enterprises, none of them export any appreciable amount of oil. Mexico and Russia have in the past been important factors in the export trade, but at the present time only Rumania has any oil for export from nationalized sources. The only important exporters, then, are the private companies.

Seven private companies control 80 per cent of the petroleum reserves outside of the United States. These same companies own a third of the domestic reserves of the United States, making their share of the world total about 70 per cent.[12] All of these companies are completely integrated and participate in all stages of the industry from exploration to marketing.

TABLE 2

PRODUCTION AND RESERVES OF THE SEVEN LARGEST OIL COMPANIES PRODUCING ABROAD

Company	1939 (Foreign) Production *	Reserves (1947) † In U.S.	Foreign	Total
Anglo-Iranian	85 million barrels	0	9.2 billion	9.2
Standard Oil (N.J.)	163 " "	2.7	5.8	8.5
Dutch-Shell	150 " "	.8	6.6	7.4
Gulf	12 " "	1.0	3.0	4.0
Texas Co.	8 " "	1.6	1.4	3.0
Standard of California	6 " "	1.4	1.2	2.6
Socony-Vacuum	14 " "	1.2	1.3	2.5
		8.7	28.5	37.2

* *Petroleum*, United States Tariff Commission, 1946.

† *World Oil*, December, 1947, p. 57. The figures are based on the more conservative estimates of Middle Eastern reserves. The reserves commonly considered as proven today would raise the share of the American companies somewhat and show the Standard Oil Co. (N.J.) to have the largest reserves in the world.

12. The reasons for the development of these very large companies to the exclusion of smaller ones are analyzed in Appendix I.

The foreign reserves and production are split about evenly between the American and the British-Dutch groups. The current holdings of the seven companies in the United States and abroad are shown in the accompanying table. It will be seen that in 1939 the vast bulk of the foreign production was in the hands of Standard Oil Company (N. J.), Dutch-Shell, and Anglo-Iranian. This pattern is changing rapidly with the growing production of the large oil reserves of the other four companies.

Until 1928 world markets and particularly the European market had been frequently marked by vigorous competition. The rise of the Dutch-Shell Company was accomplished only after a bitter struggle with the old Standard Oil Company for the European trade. In 1928, however, Shell and Jersey reached an agreement not to encroach on each other's markets.[13] The extent of this agreement and its subsequent effects are not fully known, but since then competition in the industry has been much less evident.

During the world depression and oil glut of 1932, representatives of companies owning 80 per cent of the world's producing capacity met in Paris to attempt to form a worldwide marketing agreement. Russia refused to enter, but as a result of the quotas established, prices did rise somewhat. However, Rumania did not adhere to her quota and the agreement was short-lived.[14] This seems to have been the last comprehensive attempt at world market control in petroleum.

Competition in the world market for petroleum has been limited not only because of the concentration of corporate control but also by direct participation and control on the part of governments in the consuming countries. Many foreign countries control imports of petroleum and refined products by means of quotas and discriminatory tariffs and have required American and other foreign marketing companies to

---

13. See E. Hexner, *International Cartels*, pp. 256-62, and P. H. Frankel, *Essentials of Petroleum*, p. 93, for discussions of the "As Is" agreement.

14. Plummer, *International Combines in Modern Industry*, pp. 72-77.

build refineries in non-producing countries which cannot be justified on economic grounds.[15] Because of import restrictions, limitations on the entry of new firms and a variety of other controls in most countries, the area of free competition in the marketing of the world's petroleum is severely limited.

With the development of the large potential productive capacity of the Persian Gulf area by a handful of companies which already control the bulk of the world's oil supply, concentration of control in the international market promises to be even greater in the future. Moreover, the companies in control of Middle East production have entered into agreements among themselves for the distribution of the output of the area. Large-company control over Middle East production is strengthened by the fact that marketing in the Eastern Hemisphere is also dominated by these same companies. The trend toward nationalization of the oil industry in Europe and elsewhere is the only serious threat to the position of the handful of large companies which dominate the world market.

The price system which has emerged from the control of the industry by this small oligopoly [16] has been called a basing point system, but it shows some modifications of the usual type of basing point arrangement. The United States Gulf Coast is the only point at which there is a free market for petroleum in the sense that any buyer can get crude there at the market price. The prices quoted in other parts of the world are set in relation to the Gulf price although they do not necessarily include the full amount of tankerage cost from the United States Gulf Coast. This method has been employed because the Gulf was the chief source of supply for independent importers. The purpose of a basing point system is to make c.i.f.[17] prices equal, whatever the source of supply. Recently, however, quoted prices in the Persian Gulf have

---

15. See L. M. Fanning, *American Oil Operations Abroad*, pp. 166 ff. See also the discussion in Appendix I.

16. The domination of the market by a small group.

17. Cost, insurance, and freight.

been set at or somewhat below the United States Gulf price, and it is likely that a new basing point will emerge in the Persian Gulf as it becomes a more important exporting area. At present, however, there is no free market in the Persian Gulf and each sale is by separate bids.[18]

THE OUTLOOK FOR THE FUTURE

If prewar trends continue, the world demand for petroleum and its products will be almost thirteen million barrels a day by 1955. However, in nearly every region of the world the use of petroleum is expanding at an even faster rate than before the war. Extrapolating the demand for petroleum from past trends in the United States has always produced unbelievable results. Forecasters have tended to modify their forecasts of future consumption downward and have almost invariably been wrong. The rate of increase has so far showed no tendency to decline. However, we must still be cautious in projecting the present trends into the future. Increases in the efficiency of oil-burning machinery are constantly being made, and the rise in the prices of fuel in the United States may very well slow down the rate of increase at an early date.

Extrapolation of trends for the rest of the world is on somewhat safer ground. The United States has already shown that even a nation with plentiful coal supplies can advantageously supply nearly a third of its total energy requirements from crude petroleum. Europe has been accustomed to using petroleum for less than 10 per cent of its energy. Therefore a forecast that Europe's demand will double in the next decade or less is not inconsistent with the competitive cost position of

18. In 1946 the only published price was a sale to UNRRA of several million barrels at $1.17, f.o.b. Ras Tanura. Recently, testimony before the Senate War Investigating committee has revealed that the price charged by the Arabian-American Oil Company to the Navy for its oil was $1.05 a barrel, which was considerably below the world market. Small sales were made to French buyers in 1945 at 90 and 95 cents a barrel. Testimony of J. T. Duce, quoted in *New York Times*, Oct. 31, 1947, p. 2.

the two fuels. In ten years petroleum may be cheaper i̇ Europe than in the United States, since Europe is closer to th main surplus area.

A forecast of world demand in 1955 is included in the Appendix. The world total demand which emerges from this study is twelve million barrels per day. The chief departure from prewar trends is expected to be in the United States for the reasons outlined above. The forecast assumes the absence of wars and political disturbances, no increase in trade restrictions, and no major depressions. It is thus in the nature of a maximum estimate, although the past trends on which it is based included a major depression and a considerable degree of trade restriction. This figure for world demand in 1955 is also consistent with the petroleum import goals of the Committee for European Economic Cooperation. The American petroleum industry has however expressed doubts that the CEEC petroleum consumption goals will be achieved on schedule. The heart of the problem lies in the future Middle Eastern production and the availability of facilities for transporting the oil to Europe. We will now consider this problem in detail.

CHAPTER III

THE MIDDLE EAST IN WORLD OIL PRODUCTION

Our discussion of the world petroleum market has indicated the leading role which Middle Eastern sources are destined to play. Before discussing the political and economic background of the development of these resources, we will describe in more detail the production and marketing of Middle East oil and its potentialities for the future.[1]

Although oil has long been known to exist in the Persian Gulf region, its development has been relatively slow. Large producing areas already existed closer to the principal markets, and the political difficulties involved in obtaining concessions were considerable. The major companies were therefore content to postpone the development of their concessions until the expansion of world demand made the production of Middle East oil clearly desirable from an economic standpoint. As a result, only the Anglo-Iranian Company was exporting oil as late as 1930. In Iraq production on a commercial scale had to await the completion of a pipe line to the Mediterranean in 1934, and annual production has been less than 1 per cent of the proved reserves of the Kirkuk field, one of the largest in the world.

The American companies were late comers to the Middle East. In Iraq they were bound by the wishes of their international partners and as members of the "Redline Agreement" they were forbidden to operate independently. Production on a sizeable scale from the completely American owned and

[1]. The statistics used in this chapter will be found in Tables 5 and 6 of Appendix II, where complete statistical data on Middle East petroleum are given.

26

operated concessions in Bahrein Island and Saudi Arabia did not commence until the late 1930's.

TABLE 3
PRODUCTION AND RESERVES IN THE MIDDLE EAST

Country	Discovery Date	Production (1000 b/d) 1938 *	1947 †	U. S. Share	Estimated Proved Reserve ‡ (Billions of Barrels)
Egypt	1911	4.5	26	0	0.2
Iran	1913	214.7	415	0	6–9.5
Iraq	1927	89	99	23.8%	5–7.5
Bahrein Island	1932	23	26	100	0.3
Kuwait	1938	0	45	50	5–9
Saudi Arabia	1938	1	246	100	5–7
Qatar	1940	0	0	23.8	1
		333	857	36% (1947)	23–35

* *Petroleum Data Book*, 1947.
† *Oil and Gas Journal*, July 29, 1948, p. 179.
‡ Proved reserves are variously estimated by competent authorities. Some of estimates for the major countries are as follows: (in billions of barrels).

	Iran	Iraq	Kuwait	Saudi Arabia	Total
De Golyer Report: 1945	6.5	5.0	9.0	5.0	25.5
Petroleum Data Book, 1948	7.0	5.0	9.0	6.5	27.5
Oil and Gas Journal, December 1947	9.5	7.5	5.0	6.0	28.0

The Arabian American Oil Co. now estimates proved reserves of Saudi Arabia to be 7.0 billion barrels and total reserves for the Middle East at 32 billion barrels.

Despite their late start, Americans now control about 42 per cent of the reserves of the Middle East, as compared to 52 per cent for the two British-Dutch companies, Anglo-Iranian, and Shell. Production and reserves of all the countries in which oil has been found are shown in Table 3. Although there is a variety of opinion as to the exact size of the reserves actually *proved* by drilling, most authorities quote upwards of 100 billion barrels as the *ultimate* reserves likely to be discovered in the Persian Gulf area.

Most of the known oil reserves of the Middle East lie in a long narrow zone extending about 1000 miles from Mosul in northern Iraq to Qatar on the southwestern shore of the Persian Gulf. The area favorable to oil discoveries is thought to extend farther south into Arabia and farther southeast in Iran. This region can be conveniently called the Persian Gulf area because the Tigris-Euphrates Valley which contains the northern portion is a natural extension of the Gulf. The Levantine states are much less favorable for oil occurrence, but exploration is going on in Syria, Palestine, and Trans-Jordan at the present time. The western coast of Arabia is likewise thought to be unfavorable and a concession to this territory formerly held by the Iraq Petroleum Co. group has been abandoned. The oil fields of Egypt, currently limited to the northwestern shore of the Red Sea, form a separate geological province from the Persian Gulf area. Likewise the northern provinces of Iran are geologically related to the oil fields of southern Russia rather than the Persian Gulf. So far no oil has been found in northern Iran.

Production in the Persian Gulf area almost doubled during the war, largely as a result of Allied military demand. High priority was given to refinery construction at Haifa (Palestine), Bahrein, Abadan (Iran), and Ras Tanura (Saudi Arabia). The total refinery capacity was doubled during the war and Persian Gulf refineries were able to supply the bulk of the oil requirements for the later stages of the Pacific War. They served to replace the production of the refineries in the Netherlands West Indies which were destroyed early in the war.

The 32 billion barrels of proved Middle Eastern reserves are now being produced at little over 1 per cent per year. However, because of the geology of the oil reservoirs, the maximum efficient rate in the Persian Gulf is lower than that in the United States—perhaps only $3\frac{1}{2}$ per cent as compared with more than twice this rate for the United States.[2] Even at this low annual rate, the output of the known reserves would be in excess of 3 million barrels a day, a threefold increase over current production. Since exploration of these fields has been very limited, current figures of reserves probably greatly understate the oil that will be available as the need arises.

The oil of the Persian Gulf has been found and produced very cheaply compared to similar costs in the Western Hemisphere.[3] Several factors combine to make this possible. First, the individual concessions cover large areas, and unit operation permits the employment of the most efficient methods of exploration and recovery. Second, oil is found closer to the surface, the wells generally being less than 5000 feet deep, and producing strata of 200 to 1000 feet have been found in all fields.[4] Geological conditions over much of the area are favorable to economical production, permitting a large production from a very few wells. The total reserves of the Persian Gulf area have been found by drilling less than 150 wildcat wells, while in the United States alone more than twenty times this number are drilled every year. All of these factors combine to make Persian Gulf oil the most cheaply produced in the world.

Despite these great technical advantages the exploitation of Middle East oil presents a number of difficult production problems. The major producing regions are for the most part in desert areas where climatic and other physical conditions are among the least favorable in the world. Every conceivable facility of modern industrial civilization has to be provided by the oil companies. Whole communities must be established and local laborers recruited from among primitive peoples who have no knowledge of modern methods. An important part of

2. See *Oil and Gas Journal*, May 17, 1947, p. 63.
3. Every dollar invested by American companies in Asia has produced 17 times as large reserves (mostly in the Middle East) and 3½ times as much current production as in the Caribbean area. (Investment data from *Petroleum Interests in Foreign Countries*, p. 169.)
4. Some of the wells in Saudi Arabia are as deep as 10,000 feet.

the operations of the companies consists of measures for the economic benefit of the local communities. Political instability is a constant threat. For example, Bedouin tribesmen must be bribed or combatted along the 600-mile pipe line from Kirkuk to Haifa. There are, in addition to the problems of production and refining, difficult transportation problems to be solved. Rail transportation and highways from the seaports to the fields are generally non-existent. Pipe lines must be constructed and port facilities and adequate harbors built. All of these undertakings require large amounts of capital and involve a considerable degree of risk.

WORLD MARKET FOR MIDDLE EAST PETROLEUM

Of the pre-war production of 325,000 b/d (barrels per day) in the Persian Gulf area, 230,000 b/d were exported. The greater part (75 per cent) went to Europe; the rest went to Africa and Australia. In all of these marketing areas Persian Gulf oil competed with oil from the Western Hemisphere. Persian Gulf oil, although geographically nearer to the European market than its competitors in the Caribbean-Gulf of Mexico area, is hampered by the circuitous sea route around the Arabian peninsula and the Suez Canal toll of 18 cents a barrel. This transportation disadvantage can be overcome by a shift from tanker shipments to pipe-line transportation from the producing fields to the Mediterranean. The 90,000 b/d delivered by pipe line to the Mediterranean from the Kirkuk field in Iraq is transported a shorter distance to northwestern Europe than is the oil from the Western Hemisphere.

With the completion of the projected pipe lines from the Persian Gulf area to the Mediterranean, oil from this area will have the advantage of both lower production and transportation costs over its competitors for the European market. Since the Middle East has a large potential surplus production, it is the logical supplier of the European and Asiatic markets (outside the U.S.S.R.). However, the refining capacity of the Middle East and of the Eastern Hemisphere generally cannot be expanded rapidly enough to take over this market immediately. Before the war there were only two important refineries in the Middle East: the refineries at Haifa, in Palestine, and Abadan, in Iran. During the war a new refinery at Ras Tanura in Saudi Arabia was built and the capacity of the refinery on nearby Bahrein Island expanded. The present capacity of these four refineries is about 800,000 b/d. Location of refineries near the oil fields is more economical because of the long distances from the Middle East fields to their principal markets. However, a substantial portion of the exports from this area will continue to be in the form of crude oil because of the high duties and other restrictions on the importation of refined products into many European countries. For example, American and French interests in the Iraq Petroleum Company refine their oil chiefly in France because of the high French import duties on refined products and the French import licensing system.

The development of Persian Gulf petroleum production in the next decade or so will depend largely on the growth of effective demand in the Eastern Hemisphere, particularly in Europe outside the U.S.S.R.[5] Since reserves of crude are adequate to supply almost any conceivable rate of expansion over the next few decades (assuming the availability of productive equipment and transport facilities), the problem becomes one of estimating production in other areas. Since all other sources are producing at close to capacity and may be expected to continue to do so, the Middle East forecast can be arrived at by deducting production in the rest of the world from world demand. This method gives the rate at which Middle East production will have to be expanded to keep up with developing world requirements.

On the supply side a reasonable forecast is more difficult to make than the demand forecast which was made in the preceding chapter because of the difficulty in estimating fu-

5. It is forecast that by 1955 production in the East Indies will be sufficient to supply about one third of the demand of Oceania and the Far East. See Appendix II, Table 7.

ture discoveries. Using present production rates, unused capacity, and estimated ultimate reserves, it is possible to make an intelligent guess regarding production in the Caribbean and the United States, the areas which will probably be developed to capacity to supply the Western Hemisphere. Since this estimate shows supply about equal to demand for the whole Western Hemisphere by 1955, the Middle East is left as the supplier of the rest of the world (except for the modest production of the East Indies and Russia which will probably be no more than sufficient to supply the local needs of these areas). The world deficit remaining to be supplied from the Middle East is of the order of 2½ million [6] barrels per day, and it is quite possible that the United States will be among those importing substantial amounts of oil from that area. This would represent a three-fold increase over the 1947 production of the Persian Gulf area.

The total world consumption of 12 million b/d which emerge from the calculation is considerably higher than the 9.2 million b/d which was forecast by the industry at the close of the war.[7] However, the most recent forecast by the Standard Oil Co. (N. J.) for 1951 reveals a considerably higher figure for both supply and demand,[8] and even allowing for the possibility of a world-wide depression, it seems likely that world consumption will reach almost 12 million b/d by 1955. The timing will depend more on the physical limitations of expanding production, refining, and transport facilities for Middle East oil than on the expansion of demand.

The economic feasibility of importing Persian Gulf crude to the United States at the present time depends largely on transportation costs and the availability of the Persian Gulf supply. From Table I it is evident that with the rise in the price

6. This figure includes the domestic requirements of the Middle East. See Appendix II, Table 7.

7. *Postwar Petroleum Requirements*, Hearings before the Special Senate Committee Investigating Petroleum Resources, October 3, 1945, pp. 9-11.

8. The forecast for 1951 is 9.8 million b/d excluding Russia. J. A. Cogan, *Oil and Gas Journal*, December 27, 1947, p. 158.

of east Texas crude to $2.65 per barrel by mid-1948, costs of Arabian crude and Gulf crude landed in New York were comparable even when the high U. S. Maritime Commission charter rate is used. The feasibility of importing Persian crude into the United States, even on a contract basis, is shown by the recent agreement of the American Independent Oil Company to purchase several tanker loads of Iranian crude for import.

The companies owning their own tankers and controlling sources of supply in the Middle East are in a much better position to import oil into the United States. Their profit on Arabian crude is much higher than on their domestic production, and their transport costs are much lower than the charter rate. At the present time (mid-1948) all of the production of the Arabian-American Oil Company is being taken by its four owners for their own use.[9] Two of them, Socony Vacuum and Jersey Standard, are importing some 50,000 b/d into the United States and plan to increase these imports considerably.[10]

As Middle East production is expanded and more tankers become available, imports by independent purchasers should become more generally attractive so long as the U. S. price of crude remains high. Europe will probably continue to get the great bulk of Persian Gulf production, however.

Of the 2,500,000 b/d demand for Persian Gulf crude which is envisioned for 1955, 60 to 70 per cent requires transportation through the Mediterranean as the most economical means of shipment. The new big-inch lines to the Mediterranean ports proposed for completion in the early 1950's will raise the pipe line capacity to around 1,700,000 b/d. The fact that the companies are planning immediate construction in this unsettled area shows the pressing nature of the demand. This investment in pipe lines alone will be on the order of $800 millions.

9. Statement of J. T. Duce, Vice-President of Arabian-American, quoted in *Oil and Gas Journal*, July 15, 1948, p. 56.
10. *New York Herald Tribune*, September 8, 1948, p. 34.

Present forecasts indicate that an expansion of some 200 per cent over present production rates in the Middle East will be necessary to meet the anticipated demand by 1955. Other considerations, however, raise serious doubts as to whether such a rapid expansion can be effected in the space of seven years. These considerations relate to postwar shortages of materials and dollars which make all forecasts uncertain until a definite United States program has been formulated. Although the required 2½ million barrels a day could be very quickly produced by drilling a few more wells in Iran, Kuwait, Iraq, and Saudi Arabia, this potential production is of little present value unless the equipment to handle and process the oil is available.

The existence of adequate oil reserves is only one phase of the problem of meeting the world's petroleum requirements. There are at present serious shortages of oil transport and refining capacity. Imports of crude and refined petroleum products into the United States in 1946 were more than twice the pre-war level, which when added to European imports in 1946 exceeded total imports into these areas in 1938 by a substantial margin.[11] The world's tanker capacity is already strained to meet current demands but by 1951 European requirements for petroleum imports, as estimated by the Committee of European Economic Cooperation for the countries participating in the Marshall Plan, will be nearly 1,300,000 b/d as compared with 650,000 b/d in 1938 and 570,000 b/d in 1946. In addition, United States imports may be several times their present level by 1951. The ultimate solution to this problem is the completion of the several projected pipe lines from the Persian Gulf producing areas to the Mediterranean. Oil transported to western Europe by this means needs to be carried by sea only half the tanker miles required for tanker shipment from Persian Gulf ports via the Suez Canal. But these new pipe lines cannot possibly be completed before 1951 and present completion dates may have to be re-

11. "Transport for Oil," *The Economist*, July 26, 1947.

vised by reason of material shortages and continued political disturbances in the Middle East.

Even assuming that the transport problem can be solved, Europe's petroleum requirements cannot be met without a substantial increase in refining capacity in Europe and the Middle East. The Committee of European Economic Cooperation has estimated the import requirements of the European countries participating in the Marshall Plan for refining equipment over the period 1948-1951 at $1.8 billion, about one third of which must be supplied from the United States. Even if these countries are able to obtain sufficient dollars to finance these imports, there is considerable doubt as to the ability of the United States and other countries to supply this equipment.

Assuming that the production and transportation problems can be solved, there remains the all important balance of payments problem. Once the shift of European imports from Western Hemisphere to Eastern Hemisphere sources has been completed, the drain on European dollar resources should be considerably lessened. It is expected that petroleum from both United States-owned and European-owned producing areas in the Middle East will supply petroleum to Europe. Payments to American companies will of course represent a net loss of dollars except to the extent that they are offset by expenditures by the American companies or the recipients of royalties paid by American companies outside the United States. United States companies will need to make large capital expenditures for the construction of production and refining facilities abroad, a portion of which will be spent for foreign supplies. But before the shift from Western Hemisphere sources (for which dollars must be paid almost exclusively) can be made large amounts of dollars will be required not only for increased petroleum from the Western Hemisphere and other so-called dollar sources but also for transport, refining, and production equipment. The Committee of European Economic Cooperation has estimated the dollar payments for imports of petroleum and petroleum equipment over the period 1948-1951 at $2.7 billion, of which $2.2 billion represents imports of dollar oil. Whether or not these requirements can be met will of course depend in considerable measure on the extent of American financial aid.

CHAPTER IV

THE CONCESSIONS AND THE COMPANIES

UNLIKE THE United States, most countries provide that the rights to extract the wealth of the subsoil do not follow title to the surface lands but belong to the state or in some cases to the monarch. Thus the first step in the exploration and development of a country's oil resources is to obtain a concession from the local government. In most countries where oil is found the government or its nationals do not have the capital or the technical ability to develop their own resources. Therefore they must depend upon foreign enterprise. Sometimes, as in the case of Egypt, the government becomes a substantial owner of the shares of the producing company, but even in such cases the initiative usually comes from abroad. The foreign company obtains access to the country in which oil is believed to exist by means of a concession contract with the local government. These contracts differ from country to country, but most of them have the following elements in common: [1]

(1) A definition of the area within which the company is given the right to carry on exploration and oil development.

(2) A minimum amount of drilling which must be carried on over a period of time before oil is found in commercial quantities.

(3) The duration of the concession, usually from 60 to 75 years.

(4) The financial obligation of the company in the form of lump sum payments, annual rental, royalties on each barrel

[1]. See John A. Loftus, "Middle East Oil: the Pattern of Control," *The Middle East Journal*, Vol. 2, No. 1, January, 1948, pp. 17-32.

of crude produced, and sometimes a share in the profits of the concern.

(5) A provision for supplying the oil requirements of the local economy, either free of charge or at prices below those prevailing in world markets.

(6) Installation rights and the right of eminent domain.

(7) Certain extraterritorial rights such as freedom from future taxation other than that fixed in the contract and freedom from government controls over the conditions of production and marketing.

The concession area is frequently very large,[2] sometimes covering the major part of the entire country. This permits unified operations and makes it necessary for the government to deal with only one organization. Blanket concessions are particularly significant where the company attempts to carry out economic programs for the benefit of the country as a whole. In such cases the company takes on some of the attributes of a foreign power in dealing with the local government within whose territory it operates a miniature economic empire. In its dealings with the local government the foreign company frequently cooperates closely with the government of its owners and thereby becomes an instrument of that government's national policy.

The minimum drilling requirement embodied in a number of concession contracts is for the purpose of protecting the oil producing country against being used by the concession company as an inactive reserve of petroleum. For example a company may wish to acquire additional reserves for some future development or may simply acquire a concession in order to prevent oil reserves from falling into the hands of its competitors. Since the concession contracts do not specify the rate of operations, they afford little protection against a very slow rate of development and output relative to the

---

2. The Arabian-American Oil Company's concessions in Saudi Arabia cover 440,000 square miles, and the Iraq Petroleum Company's concessions together with those of its subsidiaries cover nearly the entire territory of Iraq.

maximum rate consistent with efficient utilization of the fields. Since the bulk of the revenue obtained from granting the concession takes the form of royalties based on the output of crude, it is to the interest of the concession country to secure production at the maximum efficiency rate.

The concession contracts usually stipulate an initial lump sum payment and an annual rental payable until commercial production has begun. Thereafter royalties are paid on the net output of crude, the prevailing rate in the Middle East being 20-25 cents per barrel. The amount of royalty is generally stated in terms of gold or its equivalent in an international currency such as sterling or dollars. The overvaluation of currencies and restrictions on gold payments in recent years has led to serious controversies over the rate of payment in some instances. Some concession contracts, notably that between the Anglo-Iranian Oil Company and the Government of Iran, provide that the government granting the concession is entitled to a percentage of the profits of the oil company.[3] Since most of the concession companies are controlled by or integrated with marketing companies, the amount of their profits attributable to operations within the concession country can be manipulated so as to keep such payments at a minimum. Hence such arrangements do not appear to be especially attractive for the concession country unless the overall profit can be shared.

The concession agreements generally limit the sovereignty of the local government by stipulating that the government cannot exercise any control over the business operations of the company. Not only are the rate of production of crude and the destination, terms, and conditions of sales entirely at the discretion of the oil company, but the government gives up all claims to the foreign exchange proceeds of the exports. Finally, the companies are generally relieved of local taxation of all kinds and are given such privileges as may be necessary

3. The Anglo-Iranian Oil Company is required to pay 20 per cent of the dividends paid to the common shareholders in excess of £671,250 annually to the Government of Iran.

for the construction of facilities and the carrying on of their operations.

Generally speaking, the obligations of the concession companies to the local government do not end with the fulfillment of the letter of the contract. Most countries whose oil resources are subject to foreign exploitation tend to have rather primitive economies and frequently have unstable governments. It is therefore in the interest of the companies to aid in the development of the local economy by such measures as the provision of technical agricultural assistance, irrigation, housing, schools, recreation, and public works projects of various kinds.[4] The good will of the local community is a prime requisite to long-term successful operations of the producing companies.

IRAN

Although American interests have never been successful in establishing a concession in Iran, a brief consideration of the development of petroleum in this country is relevant to our problem since events there have tended to set a precedent for later concessions elsewhere in the Middle East.

Oil has been known in Iraq and Iran for centuries, but the demand for it was not great enough to bring prospectors until the turn of the century. In 1901 William D'Arcy, an Australian, obtained an oil concession from the Shah of Persia covering 500,000 square miles (all of Persia except the five northern provinces). The terms were very modest by present standards: an initial payment of 10,000 pounds and 16 per cent of the net profits of the concession company to the Shah. Even so, D'Arcy had difficulty in forming an exploitation company in London. Finally in 1909 he succeeded in organizing the Anglo-Persian Oil Co. Several years later the company was in need of additional capital at a time when the

---

4. For a discussion of the social and educational activities of American oil companies in foreign countries, see Petroleum Interests in Foreign Countries, pp. 271-289. See also, L. Fanning, *American Oil Operations Abroad*, Chapter XII.

CONCESSIONS AND COMPANIES 41

British Admiralty, under the leadership of Winston Churchill, was becoming interested in oil supplies, and the British Government put up two million pounds in return for 52.5 per cent of the stock of the company.

The Anglo-Iranian (its postwar name) has had a successful and profitable career. Since the first commercial well was brought in during 1908, its production has risen steadily until Iran has become the fourth largest producing country in the world and the second largest exporter. Continued exploration has revealed a number of very prolific fields, only a few of which are being exploited at the present time.

In 1932 the Riza Shah Government caused the concession to be revoked, whereupon the British Government appealed to the Council of the League, which held the concession to be binding. A new agreement, which was much more favorable to the Iranian government, was negotiated in 1933. This contract established a royalty of 4 sterling shillings per ton of crude oil produced plus an adjustment with respect to the amount by which the price of gold in London exceeds 6 pounds per ounce. In addition to this basic royalty payment the oil company agreed to pay 20 per cent of the profits in excess of £671,250, whether declared as dividends or added to reserves. The oil company is exempted from taxation by the Iranian government provided certain additional payments based on output are paid.[5] In 1946 total royalty payments including payments for tax exemption averaged 20.6 cents per barrel. By the terms of the new concession, the Anglo-Iranian also had to limit its concession to an area of 100,000 square miles. The area which it chose borders the Persian Gulf in the southwestern part of Iran. The present concession agreement terminates in 1993.

5. These additional annual payments are as follows: 9 pence per ton on the first 6 million tons and 6 pence per ton in excess of 6 million tons, for the first 15 years; during the next 15 years, one shilling per ton for the first 6 million tons and 9 pence per each additional ton. For the first 15 years the minimum annual payment is 225,000 pounds and for the second 15 years the minimum payment is 300,000 pounds.

The proved reserves of Iran are estimated at 6-9 billion barrels and are second only to Kuwait in the Middle East. Iran's 1947 production of 150 million barrels is not far behind the estimated Soviet output of 172 million with which Iran competes for third place in world production of crude. Most of Iran's crude is refined at the giant Abadan refinery which handled over 120 million barrels of oil during 1946 and is the largest refinery in the world. Anglo-Iranian plans to expand the Abadan refinery to take care of the anticipated increase in the production of crude.

Oil is believed to exist in southeastern Iran and in the five northern provinces which form a part of the Caspian Sea basin. American companies have on several occasions negotiated for concessions in Iran but they have never been successful in developing commercial production.[6] The most recent efforts were made by the Socony-Vacuum Oil Company and the Sinclair Oil Company, each of which sent representatives to Iran in the spring of 1944 to negotiate for concessions in the southeastern portion of the country. Shortly thereafter Soviet officials arrived on the scene for the purpose of obtaining concessions in the northern provinces.[7] The Soviet brought political pressure on the Iranian Government to grant a concession, but before an agreement was reached the Majlis (Iran's Parliament) passed a law (December 2, 1944) prohibiting all negotiations for oil concessions until after the withdrawal of foreign troops. This action also put an end to the negotiations by the American companies.[8]

Meanwhile continued political pressure from the U.S.S.R. for an oil concession resulted in the signing of a tentative agreement for joint Russian-Iranian petroleum development

6. In 1937 a concession covering most of northeastern Iran was granted to the Amiranian Oil Company, a subsidiary of the Seaboard Oil Company of Delaware, but the concession was abandoned the following year.

7. Russia gave up her concession in northern Iran in 1921 and acquired another during the 1930's, which was also abandoned.

8. See A. C. Millspaugh, *Americans in Persia*, The Brookings Institute, Washington, 1946.

between the Soviet Ambassador and the Iranian Premier Ghavam on April 4, 1946, while Soviet troops were still on Iranian soil. This agreement called for the establishment of a Soviet-Iranian oil company in which Russia would have 51 per cent of the voting shares for the first twenty-five years of the fifty-year term provided in its charter. After a series of diplomatic exchanges which included Soviet threats and accusations, the Iranian Majlis on October 22, 1947, voted overwhelmingly (102 to 2) to reject the tentative agreement and provided instead for a five-year petroleum exploration program from which all foreign capital would be barred.[9] In addition to prohibiting the granting of any new foreign oil concessions, the Majlis directed the Premier to negotiate with the Anglo-Iranian Oil Company for a larger share in its profits.

It goes without saying that this was a bold step for a weak nation having a common border with the U.S.S.R., and one which could not have been taken without strong diplomatic support from the United States. Shortly before the Majlis acted on the agreement the United States Ambassador George V. Allen declared that the United States would support the right of Iran to make its own choice in the matter of granting concessions to foreign powers.[10]

Although American companies are now barred from obtaining concessions in Iran, an agreement has recently been reached between Anglo-Iranian and Standard Oil Co. (N. J.) whereby the latter will purchase a substantial quantity of Iranian crude over a twenty-year period. Also involved is a proposed pipe line from the Iranian and Kuwait oil fields to the Mediterranean to be financed jointly by Jersey, Socony-Vacuum, and Anglo-Iranian. The new agreement will provide an additional source of petroleum for marketing in Europe by the two American companies to replace supplies which in the past have come from the Western Hemisphere.

9. *New York Times,* October 23, 1947, p. 1.
10. *New York Times,* September 14, 1947.

IRAQ

With the exception of a small concession in the border area adjoining Iran owned by a subsidiary of the Anglo-Iranian Oil Company, all of Iraq is under concession to the Iraq Petoleum Company and its subsidiaries. The Iraq Petroleum Company is in many respects unique in the annals of petroleum development and has probably had the most tangled history of any oil company. At different times it has included interests of seven nations and been the subject of scores of diplomatic exchanges and several international agreements. Various concessions in Mesopotamia were granted by Turkey to American, German, and British interests shortly after 1900, but frequent changes in the Turkish government prevented the development of discovery and production. In 1913 strong British Government pressure brought about the organization of the Turkish Petroleum Company to consolidate the British and German claims. Its owners included the Anglo-Persian and Dutch-Shell companies, as well as German and Turkish interests. Diplomatic pressure by Germany secured the reconfirmation of the earlier German claim to the Mosul and Baghdad concessions.

Following World War I the San Remo conference gave Germany's share in the Turkish Petroleum Company to France, and plans were made to consolidate the British, Dutch, and French interests in a single organization. During 1919 American companies tried to obtain concessions in the Mesopotamian fields but were unsuccessful in breaking the French-British hold on the area. Mention has already been made of the United States Government's protest against this policy of exclusion. After an exchange of diplomatic notes which continued over a period of five years, the British Government yielded to the American contention and agreed to give American interests a quarter share in the new Iraq Petroleum Company.[11] Following this decision seven American com-

11. H. Feis, *Petroleum and American Foreign Policy*, p. 9. See also, *Diplomatic Protection of American Petroleum Interests in Mesopo-*

panies entered negotiations for the share in the stock of Iraq Petroleum Company which was offered. The final agreement, reached in 1927, provided that the American group (reduced to five) should share equally with the Royal-Dutch, Anglo-Iranian, and the Cie. Francaise des Petroles. After several years three of the American companies withdrew, leaving the Standard Oil Company (N. J.) and Socony-Vacuum as the sole American participants. The shares owned by the two American companies are held by the Near East Development Corporation.

At present each of the following four companies owns 23.75 per cent of the shares of the IPC: (a) The Anglo-Iranian Oil Company; (b) the Royal-Dutch Shell; (c) Cie. Francaise des Petroles (35 per cent of which is owned by the French Government); (d) and the Near East Development Corporation (owned jointly and equally by Jersey and Socony-Vacuum). The remaining 5 per cent is owned by C. S. Gulbenkian, one of the owners and promoters of the old Turkish Petroleum Company. Thus the IPC represents a combination of the four largest oil marketers of the world, and the total assets of the owners exceed five billion dollars.

An important feature of this combination is the so-called "Redline Agreement" of 1928 which provided that each participant in the IPC would refrain from taking separate action in an area which included most of the old Turkish Empire. This area was to be developed only by joint action of the participants. This agreement is an outstanding example of a restrictive combination for the control of a large portion of the world's oil supply by a group of companies which together dominate the world market for this commodity. It should be said, however, that the American companies did not favor the restrictive clauses of the "Redline Agreement" but that they were forced on them by British and French interests as a condition of participation in the concession. Early in

---

tamia, Netherlands East Indies, and Mexico by Henry S. Fraser, Chief Counsel for Special Committee Investigating Petroleum Resources (S. R. 36), U. S. Government Printing Office, 1945.

1947 the "Redline Agreement" became the subject of court action by the French Government which protested that the proposal of the Standard Oil Company (N. J.) and the Socony-Vacuum to buy a share of the Arabian-American Oil Company was a violation of the 1928 agreement. The British and the American participants contended that the "Redline Agreement" was invalidated by the British Trading-With-The-Enemy Act when France became allied with Germany during the occupation.[12] The explanation of the French attitude toward independent operations of the parties to the "Redline Agreement" in the Middle East lies in the fear that France will not be able to obtain sufficient oil resources to supply her needs. All oil produced jointly by IPC is, according to the contract, shared in proportion to each participant's ownership in IPC. A satisfactory solution appears to have been reached outside of court whereby the American and British owners have agreed to a large expansion of IPC's operations in Iraq and an understanding to the effect that the American companies will make available a portion of their share of the oil produced by IPC to France in accordance with her needs.[13]

With the nullification of the restrictive clauses of the "Redline Agreement," Standard Oil (N. J.) and Socony-Vacuum are free to expand their operations in the Middle East outside of the IPC group. The proposed acquisition of shares in the Arabian-American Oil Company by Jersey and Socony together with their new sales agreement with the Anglo-Iranian will give these two American companies a substantial share in the output of Iran, Iraq, and Saudi Arabia—all of the large producing areas in the Middle East. The details of the Arabian-American purchase will be discussed in the next section.

In addition to owning oil concessions covering most of Iraq

12. See the *New York Times*, January 10, 1947. See also, "The Great Oil Deals," *Fortune*, May 1947.
13. Although the French interests have apparently dropped their suit the completion of the deal between Jersey and Socony and the present owners of the Arabian-American is at the time of writing held up by a similar suit by Mr. Gulbenkian, one of the owners of IPC.

(directly and through its subsidiaries) the IPC owns concessions in Lebanon, Syria, Palestine, Transjordan, and the sheikhdoms of Trucial Oman, Qatar, Muscat, and Hadramaut. It has received strong backing from the British Government, which in certain cases has prohibited rival companies from negotiating with local sheikhdoms over which Britain exercises political control. Since British financial interests (including the British Government which has a majority interest in Anglo-Iranian) control two of the four participating companies, Britain has a special interest in the affairs of IPC.

The terms of the IPC's concession in Iraq (which was originally granted by Turkey but later revised in 1931) provide for royalty payments at the rate of 4 shillings gold per metric ton [14] (about 22 cents per barrel) with a minimum required payment of 400,000 gold pounds ($8.24 per pound) for the first twenty years from the date of the beginning of regular exports. The company is exempt from taxation by the Iraq Government in consideration of yearly payments amounting to 9000 pounds gold up to the time of commercial export, and thereafter 60,000 pounds gold on the first four million and 20,000 gold pounds on each additional million metric tons produced.[15] For a period of twenty-five years from July 18, 1926, 10 per cent of all royalties due the Iraq Government is to be paid to the Turkish Government.

Although oil was discovered in commercial quantities in 1927, exports from the Mediterranean seaboard did not begin until 1934, following the completion of the pipe lines to the Mediterranean. Almost all production is from the Kirkuk field in northern Iraq, the reserves of which are estimated to be 5 billion barrels. Production has been considerably less than in Iran, however, because of transportation difficulties. Unlike the major producing areas of Iran and Arabia,

14. Royalties are paid in sterling calculated on the basis of the gold-sterling exchange rate in London. At the current exchange rate 4 shillings gold is equivalent to about $1.65.

15. One metric ton of crude petroleum is equivalent to about eight barrels, the exact amount depending upon the specific gravity of the crude.

the Kirkuk field in Iraq is several hundred miles from the Persian Gulf ports. A 600-mile pipe line was built by American engineers in 1934 with two branches leading to the Mediterranean ports of Tripoli (Lebanon) and Haifa (Palestine). The two British companies refine their share of the output in Haifa, while the American and French companies send their crude to Europe from Tripoli. During World War II a small refinery was built at Tripoli, which supplies the local market in Syria and another small refinery was constructed at Kirkuk. The production of the Kirkuk field has been limited to the capacity of the pipe lines, which is about 90,000 barrels a day.[16] A new 16-inch pipe line to Haifa is now under construction and plans are under way for a second 16-inch line with terminus at Tripoli. These two lines, estimated to cost $149 million, will increase the possible output of the Kirkuk field from the present 90,000 b/d to 260,000 barrels per day when they are completed in 1950.

THE ARABIAN PENINSULA

The great bulk of the American owned and controlled petroleum reserves of the Middle East are to be found in the Arabian peninsula. This territory, known as Arabia, contains about 800,000 square miles and includes the kingdom of Saudi Arabia, which accounts for about half of the entire area, Yemen, the British Crown Colony of Aden, and the various sheikhdoms and sultanates of Hadramaut, Muscat and Oman, Trucial Oman, Qatar, and Kuwait. We may also include as a part of this geographical area the important oil-producing Bahrein Island which lies a few miles off the coast of Arabia in the Persian Gulf. Out of a total of 35 billion barrels of proved oil reserves in the Middle East, about 50 per cent are found in Arabia,[17] and of the total Arabian reserves about 70 per cent are owned by American companies. The principal oil

16. *Petroleum Interests in Foreign Countries*, p. 341.
17. Arabian-American Oil Company estimate. Considerable difference of opinion exists among geologists as to the extent of the Arabian reserves. Some experts would credit Arabia with only 40 per cent of the total for the Middle East.

fields are in Saudi Arabia, Kuwait, Bahrein, and Qatar, but oil is also believed to exist in Trucial Oman which lies south of Qatar along the Persian Gulf.

Although Arabia is now thought to contain the largest share of the oil reserves of the Middle East, its exploration and development have been relatively slow. The first oil concession to be obtained in this area was on Bahrein Island by the Eastern and General Syndicate Ltd. (British), in December 1925. In 1927 a subsidiary of the Gulf Oil Corporation, the Eastern Gulf Oil Company, secured an option on the Bahrein concession from the British Syndicate after it had been examined by British geologists and declared to be unfavorable for oil occurrence. At the time the option was secured the Eastern Gulf Oil Company was a participant in the IPC and hence was a party to the "Redline Agreement" of 1928. Consequently the Gulf subsidiary had to submit its proposed concession to the Iraq Petroleum Company for approval. Although IPC was not contemplating development in this area, it prevented Gulf from securing the concession. The latter then sold its option to the Standard Oil Co. of California at cost. However, even though Bahrein was not thought to be promising, the British Government was loath to see an American company secure a foothold in the area. The British Government therefore sought to dictate the terms of the concession agreement by virtue of its political influence over the rulers of Bahrein.[18] The terms which the British proposed to the American company would have imposed a large measure of British control and were therefore not acceptable to Standard of California.

At this point the United States State Department became interested in the transaction and requested a statement of policy from the British Government regarding the granting

---

18. Although Bahrein Island is ruled by the Sheikh of Bahrein, the country is tied to Britain by a treaty which gives the latter control over its external relations, including the approval of concessions granted to foreign powers or their nationals. Britain has similar treaties with Kuwait, Trucial Oman, and Muscat and Oman.

of concessions in the semi-independent Arab states. The British Government finally decided to admit participation by American interests under certain conditions. After a year of negotiation with the British Colonial Office, the Bahrein Petroleum Co. (a Canadian subsidiary of the Standard Oil of California) was allowed to take up the concession on Bahrein Island. However, the company had to include certain British officials, and a majority of its employees had to be British subjects. The original lease covered 100,000 acres.

In 1932 the first well drilled on Bahrein Island yielded oil at a depth of 2000 feet. This discovery in an area not known to be favorable to oil stimulated interest in the neighboring territory on the mainland of Arabia and resulted in competition between IPC and Standard of California for other leases on Bahrein. Despite the pressure which the British representatives of the IPC brought to bear on the Sheikh of Bahrein, he finally agreed, in 1940, to extend the concession of the American company. The rapid development which the Bahrein Oil Co. had made of its concession was apparently the deciding factor.[19]

Shortly thereafter Standard of California sought additional concessions in the neighboring sheikhdoms of Qatar and Trucial Oman but was not successful. Although the sheikhs had indicated their willingness to negotiate, the British Government refused permission to the Americans to enter negotiations. Subsequently these areas were leased by the IPC.

The second attempt of the Gulf Oil Corporation to secure a concession in Arabia also met with political obstructions. In 1931 the British Government refused the Eastern Gulf Oil Corporation (now no longer a participant in IPC and the "Redline Agreement") permission to negotiate for a concession in the small sheikhdom of Kuwait, at the head of the Persian Gulf. The Gulf Company then appealed to the State

---

19. A further political threat to the Bahrein Company's lease is the claim of Iran to sovereignty over the island. However, the Bahrein Petroleum Company has ignored the statement of the Iranian Government that its lease is invalid.

CONCESSIONS AND COMPANIES 51

Department for aid,[20] and again the department protested to the British Colonial Office, which expressed its willingness to sanction joint participation of Gulf with a British company. In the meantime, Anglo-Iranian had become interested in the same area, and long negotiations were necessary to effect a compromise between the two companies. It was finally agreed that the two companies would share equally in the ownership of the Kuwait Oil Co., which was formed to exploit the concession.[21] However, Gulf agreed not to sell oil in any marketing area already served by the Anglo-Iranian.[22] Gulf's half interest in the concession is held by the Gulf Exploration Company of Pittsburgh.

The development of the Kuwait concession was stopped by the war after eight wells had been drilled, but operations have recently been renewed. The De Golyer Report stated that the indicated reserves in this tiny sheikhdom (6000 square miles) were nine billion barrels, the largest yet known in the Middle East. Added to those of neighboring Saudi Arabia, they make the oil reserves so far discovered in the Arabian peninsula greater than those of Texas. By the middle of 1947 Kuwait production reached 40,000 barrels a day and is expected to increase to 100,000 by 1948. No plans for local refining have been announced, but as has already been mentioned plans are underway for the construction of a pipe line from the Iran and Kuwait fields to the Mediterranean. Gulf's share of the Kuwait production is currently being sold to the Dutch Shell.

Almost simultaneously with the Kuwait negotiations, Standard of California sought to extend its concessions to the mainland of Saudi Arabia. Competition from other interests was keen there too, but fortunately for the Americans, King Ibn Saud was not under any treaty obligations to the British with respect to the granting of concessions. An earlier

20. The foreign relations of the sheikhdom of Kuwait are also subject to control by Britain through treaties.
21. *Petroleum Interests in Foreign Countries*, pp. 318-19.
22. H. Feis, *Petroleum and American Foreign Policy*, p. 33.

concession had been held in Saudi Arabia by the Eastern and General Syndicate Ltd., but it had been allowed to lapse. After the Bahrein discovery, the east-coast province of Al Hasa became very attractive as an oil prospect. British and American representatives negotiated at length with Ibn Saud before he finally decided in favor of the American company.[23] The IPC had already secured concessions in most of the Arab states surrounding Saudi Arabia, and it had strong support from the British Government in each case. It is believed that the fear of British political domination was a principal reason for Ibn Saud's selection of an American company.[24] In addition, Standard of California had already demonstrated that it could make a rapid development of its concession in Bahrein. This negotiation seems to have been practically the only case in middle eastern oil history in which the conditions approximated the standards of the "open door." The American offer was accepted on its economic merits without political intervention by either the American or the British governments.

The original concession of the California Arabian Standard Oil Co. (the new concession holder) covered 360,000 square miles along the east coast of Saudi Arabia with preferential rights to meet any other offer made for concessions covering the rest of the country. The lease was to run for sixty years and the terms called for a loan of 35,000 pounds sterling and an annual rental until the development of commercial production. The royalty established on all oil produced was four gold shillings per ton or its equivalent in dollars or sterling.[25] Western Saudi Arabia was considered the least

23. A colorful account of this negotiation is given by M. Childs in "All the King's Oil," *Colliers*, August 18, 1945.
24. *N. Y. Times*, July 15, 1933, p. 1.
25. The concession contract provides that the rate of royalty per ton of crude oil shall be either:
    (a) four shillings gold, or
    (b) dollars or sterling adjusted for changes in the exchange rate between these currencies and four shillings gold in accordance with the formula set forth in the contract.
According to the Company's calculations the current rate of royalty

favorable area for oil occurrence and was not included in the preferential area. In 1936 the IPC obtained a concession from the Saudi Arabian Government in the Hejaz and Asir provinces on terms which were considered to be quite liberal. The California Arabian Oil Company did not compete for this concession. No oil has been found there and the concession was given up.

The rest of Saudi Arabia remained unleased until 1939 although increasing international rivalry developed in the efforts to obtain a concession. All of the Axis nations made vigorous attempts to secure this source of middle eastern oil. The German minister to Iraq went to Jidda to help the Italians, who had been trying to get the concession for some time. The Japanese minister to Egypt also appeared on the scene and was reported to have offered twice as much for one-third of the area which the Americans later obtained. The omnipresent IPC also made several offers. The Arabian-American Oil Company [26] was finally successful in concluding a supplementary agreement with the King covering virtually all of the coveted area. The new agreement with Arabian-American added 80,000 square miles to the original concession and brought the total (including an option to almost all of the rest of the country) to 440,000 square miles. The area covered by the concessions is the largest exclusive concession in the world, equivalent to about one-sixth the area of the United States.

The success of the American company over its foreign competitors was received as a major victory in this country. The State Department, which had heretofore given the Arabian-American no assistance in its dealings with Saudi

---

payments should be $1.65 per ton or 22 cents per barrel when payment is made in sterling, and $1.55 per ton or 20.6 cents per barrel when payment is made in dollars. The company is currently paying in gold sovereigns at a rate of 22¢ per barrel.

26. In 1944 the California Arabian was changed to the Arabian-American Oil Co. The Texas Company acquired half interest in the concession company in 1936, the details of which will be discussed in the next chapter.

Arabia and had not even maintained diplomatic representation in the country, quickly established relations with Ibn Saud. Since then the government has established a sizeable diplomatic mission at Jidda, the diplomatic capital of Saudi Arabia, largely as a result of our interest in the development of Arabian oil resources.

Three additional concessions in Arabia are worthy of mention. One is the concession in the sheikhdom of Qatar which lies along the Persian Gulf south of Saudi Arabia. This concession, the oil reserves of which have been estimated to be 1 billion barrels, is held by the Petroleum Concessions Ltd., a subsidiary of the Iraq Petroleum Company, in which it will be recalled American companies hold approximately one quarter interest. Commercial production in Qatar has not yet begun. The other two potential concessions are the so-called Kuwait Neutral Zone which consists of a strip of territory along the Persian Gulf between the boundaries of Saudi Arabia and the sheikhdom of Kuwait, and the Iraq Neutral Zone some distance to the west between the northern boundary of Saudi Arabia and the southern border of Iraq. These zones were established by treaty in 1922 as a result of boundary disputes between Saudi Arabia and her neighbors to the north. Saudi Arabia has an equal undivided interest in each of these zones, the other half interest being held by Kuwait and Iraq respectively. Under the terms of the Supplemental Agreement of 1939 between the Arabian-American Oil Company and the Saudi Arabian Government, the company was given concession rights over Saudi Arabia's interest in the two neutral zones.[27] Although oil is believed to

---

27. The Supplemental Agreement also grants to the oil company a concession covering all of the unallotted portions of Saudi Arabia considered to have any oil possibilities, excepting the central portion of the Nedj. The agreement provided for an initial payment of 140,000 pounds gold and an annual rental of 20,000 pounds gold until oil was discovered in commercial quantities in the additional area. A payment of 100,000 pounds gold was also to be made upon the discovery of commercial production, following which royalty payments were to be made under the same terms as those in the original concession.

exist in the Kuwait Neutal Zone, little is known regarding the Iraq Neutral Zone.[28] Until an arrangement is worked out between Ibn Saud and the governments of Kuwait and Iraq regarding their respective interests in the two neutral zones, the concessions are unworkable.

At the time of writing the Sheikh of Kuwait's half interest in the Kuwait Neutral Zone is about the only area in the Middle East with good prospects of oil occurrence that has not been leased or, as in the case of the undeveloped areas of Iran, legally barred from foreign exploitation.[29] Before the war the British Government, which has important treaty rights in Kuwait, indicated that it would strongly oppose acquisition of the Kuwait half of the Neutral Zone by Arabian-American (which already has rights to Ibn Saud's half) or any other American company. Presumably, however, the terms of the Anglo-American Oil Agreement (which has not yet been ratified by the United States Senate) would bar Britain from preventing an American concession by diplomatic means.[30] Since the Arabian-American (Aramco) concession includes Ibn Saud's half interest in the Neutral Zone, presumably any concession granted by the Sheikh of Kuwait would have to be developed jointly with Aramco.

Mention has already been made of the agreement whereby Standard of New Jersey and Socony-Vacuum will acquire a 40 per cent interest in the Arabian-American Oil Company from its present owners, Standard of California and Texas.[31]

28. The Basrah Petroleum Co., an affiliate of the Iraq Petroleum Company holds the Iraq interest in the Iraq Neutral Zone.
29. One further possible source of Middle East petroleum is the underwater surface of the Persian Gulf. The gulf is shallow in many areas and is thought to be favorable for oil occurrence.
30. See Chapter IX for recent developments regarding the Kawait Neutral Zone.
31. The completion of this agreement was delayed by the suit brought by the Cie. Francaise des Petroles which claimed the proposed agreement to be a violation of the "Redline Agreement." Meanwhile Standard of New Jersey and Socony have jointly guaranteed a bank loan of $102 million to the Arabian-American Oil Company, all of which is to be paid to the present owners of the Arabian-American,

The agreement also includes participation by these two companies in the Trans-Arabian Pipeline Company in the same proportion as their interest in Arabian-American, i.e., 30 per cent by Standard Oil Co. (N. J.) and 10 per cent by Socony-Vacuum, the remaining 60 per cent being divided between Standard of California and Texas. Construction costs for the Trans-Arabian pipe line, now estimated at $225 million, will be financed by a loan from a group of eight insurance companies, the loan being guaranteed by the four owners of the pipe-line company in proportion to their participation.

EGYPT

Oil was discovered in Egypt in 1911 and her production played an important part in supplying Britain's petroleum needs during World War I. Since then Egypt has not proved to be especially fertile for oil exploitation. Several small fields have been discovered, and in 1938 the important Ras Gharib field on the Red Sea was brought into production, which now accounts for over 90 per cent of Egypt's production. The original Gemsah field is now nearly exhausted. The oil producing properties are owned by the Anglo-Egyptian Oil Fields, Ltd., whose owners include the Royal-Dutch Shell, the Anglo-Iranian, and the Egyptian Government. Two groups of American companies hold extensive oil concessions in

---

the Standard of California and the Texas Companies, in repayment for advances made to their subsidiary and as dividends. As soon as the arrangements for direct participation in the Arabian Oil Co. are completed, Jersey and Socony will repay the bank loan and receive 30 per cent and 10 per cent respectively of the shares in the Arabian-American. The proceeds of the loan are being used to retire the advances made by the parent companies of Aramco during the first fourteen years of the company's life (reported to have totalled $80 million). In addition to the $102 million already advanced in the form of guaranteed loans, Jersey and Socony are reported to have agreed to pay $138 million out of future production or a total of $240 million for their 40 per cent interest in Aramco. The company was organized in 1933 with a capital of $700,000 and its total assets were reported at $150 million in 1947.—"The Great Oil Deals," *Fortune*, May, 1947, p. 175.

CONCESSIONS AND COMPANIES 57

Egypt, but thus far none of these has produced oil in commercial quantities.[32] Standard Oil Co. (N. J.) has concessions in the Red Sea area. Each group owns concessions covering six million acres, the maximum permitted to any one company under Egyptian law. Drilling operations were interrupted by the war but have now been resumed.

OTHER CONCESSION AREAS

The three remaining middle eastern countries in which petroleum concessions are held are Transjordan, Palestine, and Syria. Concessions in all three of these countries are held by subsidiaries of the Iraq Petroleum Company. Petroleum Development (Trans-Jordan) Ltd., an IPC subsidiary, was recently granted a 75-year exclusive concession to explore and develop oil and gas resources in Transjordan, and the company has agreed to drill the first test well within eighteen months. In addition to a bonus of £50,000 to the kingdom of Transjordan for granting the concession and annual rental payments increasing from £15,000 for the first three years to £80,000 after fifteen years, the company has agreed to pay a royalty ranging from about 15 cents per barrel at 20 degrees gravity to about 22 cents per barrel at 35 degrees. Once oil is produced in commercial quantities, royalty payments are to be deducted from annual rental payments.[33]

Exploratory drilling has also begun in the Negeb, a desert area in southern Palestine and some exploration has been carried on in Syria since before the war. As yet, however, oil in commercial quantities has not been discovered in any of the three countries. Exploration in neighboring Turkey has likewise yielded little returns.

32. The South Mediterranean Oil Fields, Ltd., formerly owned jointly by Standard of California and the Texas Company, holds concessions in the western desert northwest of Cairo and on the Sinai peninsula, but the American companies recently sold out their interests.
33. *Wall Street Journal*, July 29, 1947.

CHAPTER V

AMERICAN PETROLEUM DEVELOPMENT IN BAHREIN AND SAUDI ARABIA

SINCE OUR PRINCIPAL interest lies in the realm of economic and political policy rather than in the technical aspects of Middle East petroleum production, the discussion of petroleum operations will be limited to a brief sketch of the experience of the wholly American-owned companies operating in Saudi Arabia and the neighboring Bahrein Island. From the American point of view, these areas are of primary importance, since they contain the largest United States-owned reserves and the concessions are entirely operated by American companies. The potential reserves of Saudi Arabia are thought to be the largest in the Middle East, and they are undergoing the most rapid expansion of any field in the world.

Although the Bahrein Petroleum Co. is legally a separate organization, it operates as a unit with the Arabian-American in many respects and two American firms are joint owners of both companies. It is, therefore, convenient to treat the two companies together. The technical problems of exploitation will be considered first, followed by a discussion of the economic problems which are posed by the development.

TECHNIQUES OF DEVELOPMENT

After the discovery of commercial reserves in a new area, several years are required before production, transportation, and marketing facilities can be set up. After that, production may rise rapidly. For the Bahrein-Saudi Arabia operation, this period of development lasted from 1932 until 1939. The discovery of oil practically at tidewater made transportation much less of a problem than in most new developments and shortened considerably the preliminary period.

Representatives of the Standard of California arrived in Bahrein in 1930. A year later drilling began, and in June 1932 the first well was completed as a producer at a depth of 2,000 feet. Where the Anglo-Iranian engineers had decided against drilling, the American company struck oil on the first test. Whether due to superior skill or plain luck, this strike was portentous for Arabian oil development. The Bahrein field developed steadily until a production rate of 20,000 barrels a day was attained in 1937. Seventy-four wells have been drilled on Bahrein with no dry holes. But since 1939 very few wells have been drilled, chiefly because of the desire to employ the available materials and manpower for operations in the richer fields on the mainland of Arabia.

Geologically Bahrein Island is the surface reflection of a "structural high," from which the strata dip downward in all directions. Although the significance of this fact for oil occurrence was probably recognized by geologists long ago, the region failed to attract attention because the exposed layers are older than those previously known to contain oil in the Middle East. Drilling was commenced after only surface mapping, but a fortunate selection of the initial site made the discovery cost of the field only $650,000 for drilling.[1]

Geological work on the mainland of Saudi Arabia started immediately after the concession was secured by the California Arabian Oil Company in 1933. Surface exploration revealed a favorable geological structure, the Dammam dome, opposite Bahrein Island and several others extending north and south from there. Drilling required considerable preparation, since there were no settlements in the area and no labor available. Drillers, engineers, and construction men were brought from the United States, and considerable preliminary work in setting up a construction camp in the desert had to be done before drilling commenced. Permanent buildings were erected to enable the Americans to withstand the heat.

The first wells drilled in Saudi Arabia were disappointing.

1. *Petroleum Interests in Foreign Countries*, p. 379.

The structure was similar to that of Bahrein, but oil was not found in commercial quantities. After ten wells had been drilled at the level of the Bahrein wells, it was decided to test deeper. Three years after drilling had started major reserves were established at a depth of 4,700 feet. Subsequently thirty-three wells have been completed in the Dammam field, and until the recent development of the Abqaiq field it supplied the bulk of Saudi Arabian production.[2] Since the concession area is so vast, a great amount of geological work remains to be done in Saudi Arabia. A large amount of triangulation had to be done in addition, since the country has never been surveyed. Subsurface geophysical methods are very important because the strata are only slightly deformed and surface methods are quite inadequate. A start has been made with seismograph and gravity surveys, supplemented by structure drilling. Geologists have to work under extreme conditions of heat and isolation and must be accompanied by soldier escorts and guides. Despite the substantial progress which has been made, a great deal more remains to be done before an accurate estimate of the amount of oil in Arabia can be made.

As a result of these explorations, four other commercial fields have been found within a hundred miles of the Dammam field. Of these the Abqaiq field, fifty miles to the southwest, is expected to be the chief source of supply for the new refinery at Ras Tanura. The proved reserves of the Abqaiq field are over 3 billion barrels but its extent is as yet undetermined. Twenty-five producing wells have been completed in this field and current production is averaging 200,000 barrels per day. The Abu Hadriya and Qatif fields are still in the exploratory stage, but major reserves have been established in all three. Total reserves were estimated in 1944 by De Colyer at 4 or 5 billion barrels,[3] but

2. Arabian-American Oil Co., *Summary of Middle East Oil Developments*, 1948.
3. *Preliminary Report of the Technical Oil Mission to the Middle East to the Petroleum Reserves Corporation* by E. De Golyer, Chief of Mission, February 1, 1944. De Golyer now estimates Saudi Arabian reserves at 5-7 billion barrels.

more recent discoveries indicate proved reserves of 7 billion barrels. At the end of 1947 about sixty wells had been completed in the four fields with a daily average production of 305,000 barrels, and by mid-1948 production had been increased to 425,000 b/d.

Commercial production in Dammam began in September 1938 with shipment by barge to Bahrein for refining. A difficult transportation problem was created by the fact that the coast has no harbor deep enough for ocean-going tankers. The company undertook an extensive hydrographic survey, with the assistance of the British Admiralty, to find a suitable harbor. As a result, a sandspit called Ras Tanura, forty miles north of Dammam, was chosen as the most suitable spot for a port. Even there, tankers can only approach the shore by a circuitous channel. By 1939 pipe-line and storage facilities had been completed at Ras Tanura and the first tanker of crude oil was loaded. This milestone was made the occasion for a great festival, attended by King Ibn Saud and many of his official household. A caravan of 2,000 people journeyed across the desert in 400 motor cars and set up camp near the new company settlement and the King took the opportunity to inspect all the company's operations.

Until recently all the local refining of both Bahrein and Saudi Arabian crude was done on Bahrein Island. During the war this refinery was selected by the Allies for enlargement because of its strategic location, and its capacity was raised to 135,000 barrels a day. In 1945 an underwater pipe line was constructed from Bahrein Island to the mainland to bring in Arabian crude for refining. Another wartime project of great importance was the construction of a large refinery at Ras Tanura. The chief function of this refinery during the war was to supply the navy with diesel and fuel oil. Building this refinery under war conditions of supply in a remote corner of the world was a major achievement.[4] Fifteen hundred Italian workers were brought in to supplement the 10,000

4. As an example of the engineering problems encountered, 120,000 gallons of water an hour are required for cooling.

Arabs and 650 Americans employed. Since the only local materials available for construction work are sand and rock, everything else had to be imported. A dock 2400 feet long was built to load tankers. The refinery, which attained full utilization at the end of 1945, has a capacity of about 130,000 barrels per day.

The present capacity of the two refineries at Bahrein and Ras Tanura is somewhat less than the combined production of the Arabian and the Bahrein fields, now established at over 400,000 barrels per day. By 1952 production from the Saudi Arabian fields alone is expected to be over 700,000 barrels per day. A substantial portion of this output may, however, be sold as crude, especially since many European countries are planning to do their own refining. Although oil production in Saudi Arabia is still small in comparison to its reserves, output is now second only to Iran in the Middle East and fifth among the oil producing countries of the world.

PERSONNEL

The Persian Gulf is one of the most uncomfortable places in the world for people from the temperate zones. The intense heat of the desert, rising as high as 130 degrees, is combined with the humidity from the nearby Persian Gulf. The oil companies must therefore provide considerably more than the usual oil-field camp facilities to induce the workers to live there. For their American and British employees, the Bahrein and Arabian-American companies furnish air-conditioned living quarters, restaurants, clubs, and all the customary facilities of western life. Consequently, the American companies have had little trouble in recruiting technicians to work in this isolated and uncomfortable spot. The returns in improved health and efficiency have been worth the expense involved.

Far more difficult is the securing and training of native laborers which constitute the bulk of the companies' personnel. The Bahrein company had to bring in semi-skilled workers from Iraq and India, whose nationals fulfill the requirement of the concession contract that a maximum of the employees must be British subjects. Bahrein Island is more thickly settled than Arabia, and consequently it has more available native labor. Bahreinis were trained to replace the imported clerks and semi-skilled workmen and now comprise more than two-thirds of the Bahrein company's employees. When the Arabian development began, many Bahreinis were taken over to the mainland. Since the area of the company's operations is largely sandy desert with very few settlements, Arab labor was scarce. Artisans had to be imported from Jidda on the East coast and elsewhere in the Middle East.

That native employees in the Persian Gulf area can become highly skilled technicians after proper training has been demonstrated by the progress of the Anglo-Iranian operations in Iran. At Abadan 35,000 Iranians are employed and many of them are trained in company schools.[5] A technical institute has been established by the company to train the most promising students to be engineers and at present 350 natives are taking advanced training. Schooling is planned in cooperation with the Iranian government and has materially aided the company's employees.

At present the Arabian-American employs over 15,000 native workers and its local payroll is about $500,000 per month. The beginning rate of pay is 90 cents per day but several times this rate can be earned by the more experienced and efficient workers. Time and a quarter is paid for overtime and bonuses based on length of service are granted to each worker who has been in the company's service over one year. These rates of remuneration, together with paid vacations and various health, recreation, and educational services provided by the company were unheard of in Arabia before the oil was found.

A beginning has been made in setting up a training program similar to that in Iran. In 1943 an American educator was brought in to superintend the company's expanding school system and a program of hiring students on a part-time basis was started with a view to securing a higher percentage of literate employees. The company provides housing, medical

5. *Oil and Gas Journal*, August 10, 1946, p. 61.

service, and various sickness and accident benefits in an effort to secure more efficient workmen.[6] Since the number of employees in petroleum production is small compared to the capital employed, such employee benefits can economically be undertaken in the interests of improved operation.

MARKETING ARABIAN OIL

By 1936 production on Bahrein Island had reached commercial proportions (12,000 b/d), and Standard of California, which at that time was the sole owner of the Bahrein Petroleum Company, was in need of marketing facilities. To have attempted to compete with other established companies in the area would have involved years of effort and large expenditures on a marketing organization. However, the Texas Corporation had extensive marketing facilities [7] throughout Asia and Africa which it had been supplying from United States sources. It was not difficult for the two companies to reach an agreement to merge their interests "East of Suez" with substantial advantages to both. The consolidation agreement provided that each should have an equal share in all ventures in this area. A new company, the California Texas Oil Co., Ltd. (Caltex), was organized as a subsidiary of the Bahrein Petroleum Company to own the marketing subsidiaries [8] of the Texas Corporation. At the same time Standard of California was given an option on half interest in the Texas Corporation's marketing facilities in Europe.[9] In the same

---

6. *Petroleum Interests in Foreign Countries*, pp. 286-87.
7. The book value of the Texas marketing subsidiaries in Asia and Africa was 27 million dollars.
8. Cf. J. Moody, *Manual of Investments (Industrials)*, 1945 ed., p. 1738. The Texas Company's marketing subsidiaries involved in marketing East of Suez are the Texas Company (India) Ltd., The Texas Company (South Africa) Ltd., The Texas Company (Philippine Islands) Inc., The Texas Company (China) Ltd., and the Texas Company (Australasia) Ltd.
9. In December 1946 these European marketing facilities were purchased by Caltex from the Texas Company for $28 million, Standard of California's option having been allowed to lapse in 1939. See "The Great Oil Deals," *Fortune*, May, 1947, p. 175.

year the Texas Corporation acquired half interest in the California Arabian Oil Company, holder of the Saudi Arabian concession, from the Standard of California. As a result of this merger, Arabian oil is marketed throughout Europe, Africa, and the Far East. Without the acquisition of these established market outlets the development of Arabian oil might have been much slower. In addition to a ready market, the resources of the Texas Co., one of the largest oil companies in the world, were added to those of the Standard of California in the development of the concessions.

THE NEW PIPE LINES

A significant phase in the current development of middle eastern oil is the construction of pipe lines to save the long tanker trip around the Arabian peninsula. All of the Persian Gulf fields are within a thousand miles or so of the eastern Mediterranean, but the tanker trip from the Gulf by way of the Suez Canal is about 3,600 miles. Both from short- and long-run points of view pipe lines are the most economical means of shipping crude to the west.[10] The president of the new Trans-Arabian Pipeline Co. estimates that the cost of transportation from Abqaiq to the Mediterranean by pipe line will be one-third of the present tanker cost.[11] In view of the present critical steel shortage the construction of pipe lines has an additional advantage. The pipe line now being built from Saudi Arabia requires only two-thirds as much steel as its equivalent in tanker capacity. Moreover, since oil is the most crucial item in the European Recovery Program after food, its movement to Europe should have a high priority.

There are four or five large pipe lines proposed for the transport of oil to the Mediterranean from the Persian Gulf fields, but only two are beyond the planning stage at the time

10. See the Appendix for a discussion of the economies of pipe-line transportation.

11. B. E. Hull, in a paper before the American Petroleum Institute reprinted in the *Oil and Gas Journal*, November 15, 1947.

this is being written. The route of the line between the Abqaiq field in Saudi Arabia and Lebanon has been surveyed and construction is already under way. The line will be 1067 miles long, comparable to the "Big Inch" line in the United States, but considerably larger in diameter. It will transport 300,000 barrels of crude per day and this capacity can be raised to 500,000 by the installation of more pumping stations. The present proposed terminus of the line is Sidon in southern Lebanon and completion is scheduled for 1950.

The construction of the Abqaiq-Lebanon line is another example of the gigantic scale upon which almost everything connected with Middle East oil is being done. The pipe is being rolled in a steel mill in California, built especially for the purpose. The total shipping contract for transporting the equipment for the line is reported to be the largest private peacetime marine contract ever undertaken. Some 2,000 Americans are being sent to Arabia to supervise the various phases of installation. The demand for unskilled labor is expected to create a shortage in Arabia and the Near East. Total cost is estimated at $225,000,000.

The other three lines are on much the same scale. The route of the proposed 800-mile line between Iran and Lebanon has not yet been selected, but the starting capacity is set at 500,000 b/d. The line may also tap the Kuwait field unless a separate line is built by the Kuwait Oil Company. Construction by the Middle East Pipeline Company is tentatively set for 1949, with the pipe to be rolled at the same California mill. A third pipe-line system is planned to connect the Kirkuk field in Iraq with Haifa and Tripoli, duplicating the two lines already in existence. The lines will have a combined capacity of 175,000 barrels per day. Completion of the Haifa branch is scheduled for 1949 and the Tripoli branch for 1951, but progress is governed by the availability of the steel pipe which is being manufactured in England. Still another pipeline system connecting Haifa and Tripoli with the Kirkuk fields is being planned for the future. The new system is expected to add another 300,000 barrels per day to the two systems already in existence or under construction. See Table 8, Appendix II, for details of all the lines.

The completion of these four lines will raise pipe-line delivery capacity between the major Middle East fields and the Mediterranean from its present 90,000 b/d to around 1,700,000 b/d. This is about the estimated demand of western Europe alone by 1951, but in view of the shortages of critical materials, it is doubtful whether these lines will be completed before 1953 or even later. The cost of these pipe-line projects will be on the order of 800 million dollars, considerably more than half of which will be financed by American companies. Since pipe lines are normally amortized over a longer period than most other types of equipment, their construction indicates a long-term commitment to produce and sell oil more clearly than any contract. This fact is especially significant in the light of the recent sales agreement involving the Anglo-Iranian and the two American companies, Jersey and Socony. It is also interesting to note that the Iran-Kuwait-Lebanon line which will be financed jointly by Anglo-Iranian and the two American companies will tap the Kuwait field operated jointly by Anglo-Iranian and Gulf.

FOREIGN EXCHANGE PROBLEMS

A major problem of all American companies operating and marketing abroad is the widespread existence of exchange controls. American companies operating in Iraq, Kuwait, Egypt, and Bahrein have had the same exchange problems as all Americans within British-controlled areas since 1939 when sterling-area exchange controls were established. However, exchange restrictions have thus far not seriously hampered the operations of the oil companies because of the world-wide shortage of petroleum. In some cases, oil has had to be supplied from sterling areas rather than more economic dollar sources, but during the war there was such an acute shortage of oil that the source of supply was of secondary importance. Although dollar receipts from oil exports from Bahrein and other sterling countries had to be turned over to the London authorities, the priority on refined products was so high that dollars were generally made available for necessary purchases. Dollars were also released for the construction of new refinery capacity in Bahrein. Once the current world shortage of petroleum is relieved, however, exchange controls threaten to hamper American operations in several ways. First, oil produced by American companies in the Middle East and sold for dollars may be discriminated against in favor of oil sold by British or French companies for sterling or francs. American companies must sell a large portion of their oil for dollars in order to pay dividends to American owners and buy equipment and supplies which can only be obtained in the United States. Royalties may usually be paid in dollars or sterling but they have been customarily paid in dollars. If and when sterling again becomes generally convertible into dollars [12] American companies will be able to accept sterling instead of dollars. The knowledge that a large part of the sterling paid to American companies will be immediately converted into dollars may result in a continuation of discriminatory controls in areas under British influence. Similarly there may be discrimination against American oil sold in the franc currency area or in countries which find it easier to obtain francs than dollars.

A second exchange problem for American companies arises in cases where the companies are subject to exchange restrictions imposed by the government of the country in which the concession is held. This is not true in Saudi Arabia and Kuwait, but exchange controls do affect company operations in Bahrein, Egypt, and Iraq. Exchange control regulations frequently require companies to turn over all foreign exchange acquired from exports to the governmental authorities, and to obtain the dollars which they need for the

---

12. The Anglo-American Financial Agreement provided that all sterling receipts arising out of current international transactions shall be free from restrictions on transfer and convertibility after July 15, 1947. However, the British government was forced to suspend convertibility on August 20, 1947.

payment of dividends and the purchase of equipment and supplies only under license from the central authorities. Controls may limit the ability of the companies to purchase American equipment and supplies which in the petroleum field at least are regarded as the best in the world. In the past exchange controls have also limited the making of dividend and amortization payments to foreign owners. It is for this reason that many concession contracts provide that the proceeds from exports remain in the hands of the companies and may not be sequestered by the government of the concession country and that there may be no interference with imports for the account of the concession company. This is the situation in Saudi Arabia, but this country has its own peculiar currency problems which will be discussed in the next chapter.

PROFITS AND ROYALTIES

The Saudi Arabian oil development is unique in that it involves very few of the usual problems of foreign economic penetration. It does not compete with any local industry for labor or markets. It performs a service to the country which can only be performed by a foreign group at the present time. If the Arabian-American (or some other foreign company) did not produce the oil, it would probably remain undiscovered under the sands of Arabia as it has for thousands of years. Since there is no scientific method of determining what share of the economic rents should go to the landowner and what share to the concession-holder, any accusation of exploitation can only be relative.

The current rate of royalty of 22 cents per barrel paid to the Saudi Arabian Government compares favorably with most of the royalties paid by other concession holders in the Middle East. Other rates are as follows: Iran, 20-22 cents; Iraq, 22 cents; Bahrein, 14 cents; and Kuwait, 13 cents. However, the rates paid to Caribbean countries are somewhat higher. (The Venezuelan royalty rate plus taxes was 35 cents per barrel in 1946). It is difficult to judge the adequacy of these rates in relation to profits. The risks involved in foreign operations of this kind are great and the companies have had to invest large sums for many years before realizing any returns. Up to the end of 1946 Aramco had invested $120 million and is planning to invest several hundred millions more over the next decade. In 1946 net profits on sales of $18 million were $5 million. The company has paid no dividends out of earnings in the fourteen years of its operations. The potential profits on the anticipated rates of production at current crude prices are enormous but it is too early to judge them in relation to royalties and their adequacy for attracting additional capital into the industry. The matter of royalties will have to be determined in relation of rates paid by other concession holders in other parts of the world and of course by the relative bargaining strength of the concession holders and the governments of the producing countries.

A more significant question has to do with the effects of the oil industry on the welfare of the common people of the country. This problem will be explored in the following chapter.

CHAPTER VI

THE IMPACT OF OIL ON THE ARABIAN ECONOMY

THE SUDDEN INTRODUCTION of a large modern industrial enterprise into a primitive desert community must inevitably have far-reaching repercussions upon the economic and social life of the inhabitants.[1] Nowhere is this more apparent than in Saudi Arabia,[2] which until a few years ago was almost completely isolated from any contact with the Western world. The employment of thousands of native workers in the oil fields and refineries involves not only their learning modern industrial techniques but also an acquaintance with western modes of living. The sudden increase in the revenues of the country is accompanied by the development of public works, modern communications systems, industrial and agricultural development, and larger imports of industrial commodities of all kinds. The economic contact with the outside world requires the introduction of banking, foreign exchange, and trading facilities which were almost unknown in the country a few years ago. Along with these economic changes will come a social and political transformation. Modern industrial communities cannot long be governed by tribal chieftains more or less under the control of an absolute monarch. Social customs with respect to women, the relations between the individual and his tribe, individual liberties, and

---

1. For an excellent study of economic and social conditions in Saudi Arabia see K. S. Twitchell, *Saudi Arabia* (Princeton, N. J.: Princeton University Press, 1947).
2. The social contrast between Western and Arabian cultures is exemplified by the fact that King Ibn Saud in a recent visit to Dhahran met women socially (in the Western sense) for the first time in his life.

perhaps even religion will undergo a change when the desert Arabs forsake tending their flocks and work for wages in industrial communities or on large farms. But before exploring further the impact of oil on the Arabian economy let us look briefly at the economic and political organization as it exists at the beginning of this transformation.

THE ECONOMIC AND POLITICAL STAGE

Saudi Arabia is unique among the members of the United Nations. Politically the country has advanced little since the days of the Prophet. Its territory of a half million square miles and population of 4.5 million are governed by an absolute monarch, Ibn Saud, who maintains power by means of military force supplemented by his influence as a religious leader and by subsidies to the tribal chieftains. Before World War I Saudi Arabia was a part of the Ottoman Empire but was never very securely held by the Turks. Local rule was in the hands of sheikhs and tribal chieftains who maintained varying degrees of allegiance to the Sultan of Turkey. Ibn Saud carved out by the sword the country which bears his name. King Abdul Aziz Ibn Abdur Rahman al Faisal al Saud was the son of Abdur Rahman who at the time of Ibn Saud's birth in 1880 was ruler of the Nejd, a large area in central Arabia. While Ibn Saud was a boy his father was driven out of the Nejd by the Rashidi, who conquered the Nejd and its capital Riyadh, forcing Abdur Rahman and his family into exile in Kuwait. When he was twenty-one (1901) Ibn Saud organized a small force and conquered Riyadh, driving out the Rashidi. After a series of campaigns against the Turks and the Rashidi, Ibn Saud became complete master of the Nejd by the end of 1906. Another campaign against the Turks on the eastern coast brought the large province of Hasa under his rule in 1913.

During World War I the British, through the exploits of the legendary Lawrence of Arabia, joined forces with Hussein, The Sherif of Mecca, against the Turks and drove them out of the Hejaz, a province containing the Holy cities of Mecca and Medina. Following the war Hussein became King of the Hejaz and his sons Faisal and Abdulla subsequently became the local rulers of the British mandates of Iraq and Transjordan, respectively. Shortly thereafter Ibn Saud waged war on King Hussein and in 1924 captured Mecca, driving its ruler into exile. The following year Ibn Saud completed his conquest of the territory now included in Saudi Arabia by conquering the remainder of the Hejaz.

For many centuries the basic unit of government in Saudi Arabia has been the tribe, with rule centered in the tribal chieftain. Before Ibn Saud welded the tribes into a nation, the country was divided into four more or less independent kingdoms, each of which maintained some measure of control over the tribes within their borders. The former kingdoms are now the provinces of Nejd, Hejaz, Hasa, and Asir, each of which is governed by a viceroy appointed by the King. Two of these provinces, Nejd and Hejaz, are governed by sons of Ibn Saud and the other two are also governed by relatives of the King. The cities and villages are governed by amirs who act both as administrators and judges. The basis of the legal system is Koranic law and the theologians play an important part in assisting and advising the governors in legal and judicial matters. Western democratic institutions are practically unknown but officials from the amir of the smallest village up to the King are generally accessible to the poorest Arab in the land. Rule is in general benevolent and paternalistic, and decisions are not arbitrary but must be firmly grounded in tradition and religious law.

Economically Saudi Arabia is one of the most primitive countries in the world. A large part of the population consists of wandering tribes whose occupation is tending herds of camels, sheep, and goats. In the towns, which are generally located on the oases, production and trade are carried on in much the same way as they were in medieval times. The principal cities are: Riyadh, the capital (population 25,000); Mecca, the holiest city of the Moslem world (population 40,000); Medina, the second holiest city (population 20,000);

and Hofuf (population 100,000-200,000). The chief port and residence of foreign diplomatic representatives is Jidda on the Red Sea. A new town of Dammam which has recently been built by the Arabian-American Oil Company is expected to become an important Persian Gulf port.

The townspeople are principally merchants, artisans, and gardeners who work in the nearby fields. The cultivable land around the oases towns is largely owned by a few wealthy landholders who rent the fields, usually for a fixed amount of the produce. The most important professional class is the religious teachers who conduct services in the mosques and have certain judicial functions under Moslem law. Native industry is largely in the handicraft stage. Wool weaving is perhaps the best organized industry since it requires the employment of capital for the hand-operated looms. Much of the weaving is done in small factories with the workers being paid piece-rate wages. Other handicraft trades include wool spinning, tailoring, crude tanning, tile and pottery making, soap making, simple iron mongering, crude jewelry manufacturing, and the production of kitchen utensils, swords, and daggers. Most of the production is carried on by artisans working in small shops and frequently producing to order. None of these commodities is exported and in almost no industrial field is production sufficient to meet local needs.[3]

Saudi Arabia, except for the mountainous portion of the southern border, is one of the most arid plains in the world. There are, however, oases where fruits, vegetables, and grains can be grown, and even parts of the desert have sufficient rainfall to provide food for flocks of camels, sheep, and goats.

3. The only modern industry in Arabia other than oil is gold mining. In 1932 gold was discovered about 250 miles north of Jidda and the government granted a concession to the Saudi Arabian Mining Syndicate to exploit all of the mineral wealth of the country except oil. The Syndicate is owned by British, American, and Canadian interests with 25 per cent of the shares held by the Saudi Arabian Government and a few of its nationals. About one million dollars worth of gold concentrates plus small amounts of silver, lead, and copper are produced annually.

The most important crop is dates, which form the staple diet for 80 per cent of the population. Some wheat and barley are grown but not nearly enough for minimum local requirements. Alfalfa and a great variety of fruits and vegetables are also raised. The bulk of this cultivated land is to be found on or near the oases where water may be brought up from wells and led through ditches to irrigate the rows of date palms and other crops. Irrigation methods are quite primitive, the water being brought up in skin baskets by means of a crude mechanism powered by animals. Surveys by foreign engineers have shown that by a proper utilization of ground waters the area of cultivation could be substantially extended. There is need for modern pumping equipment in many areas which now depend upon camels and donkeys for irrigation.[4]

Saudi Arabia is dependent upon imports for nearly all manufactured commodities and a large share of her basic foodstuffs. It is for this reason that royalties and other foreign exchange payments by the oil company have a special significance for the Arabian economy. Aside from oil and the pilgrimage traffic, Saudi Arabia has few exports from which she can derive the necessary foreign currencies to pay for her essential imports.[5] Although no trade statistics are published, Saudi Arabia's imports for the year 1945 are estimated to be about $17 million.[6] The most important imports are cereals, sugar, textiles, tea, and automotive, radio, and farm equipment. Saudi Arabia is not even self-sufficient in dates, her most important agricultural crop, and in normal times imports dates from Iraq.

Communications in this vast desert area are extremely poor.

---

4. The most fertile portion of Saudi Arabia is the province of Asir in the southwest corner bordering Yemen. Here there is intermittent cultivation of dura over an area of some 6,000 square miles, and in the region along the Red Sea is found the bush from which oil of myrrh is derived, an important Saudi Arabian export.

5. In addition to petroleum and gold concentrates Saudi Arabia exports small amounts of charcoal, hides and skins, and essential oils.

6. "Saudi Arabia," *International Reference Service*, Department of Commerce, August, 1946.

Except for the roads built by the oil company to serve its operations on the Persian Gulf, there are only forty-five miles of surfaced highway in the country, the road from Jidda to Mecca over which the pilgrims are transported. The remainder are either poor dirt roads or mere tracks in the desert, the use of which makes trucks and cars operating in Arabia subject to rapid deterioration and high maintenance costs. It is possible to travel by truck or car between most of the cities although such trips are extremely arduous. In 1939 there were 1100 trucks and 500 motor cars in Saudi Arabia, but there have been few replacements during the war. There is an airport at Jidda and regular air service between Jidda and Cairo. There is also air service between Bahrein, Cairo, and India and between Jidda, Riyadh, and Dhahran. In 1946 the United States Army completed an airfield at Dhahran in the heart of the oil producing region on the Persian Gulf. By agreement with Ibn Saud this airport will be occupied by American military personnel for a period of three years, after which it is to be turned over to the Saudi Arabian Government, but it will be operated by American civilian personnel.[7] The new airport will be used by TWA in its through flight to and from India.

WARTIME FINANCIAL DEVELOPMENTS

Financial developments in Saudi Arabia during the war reveal a growing interest on the part of the United States Government in the economic problems of this important oil-producing country. Although Saudi Arabia was not a base of military operations during World War II, it was an important link in the chain of sea and air communications to the Far East, and, in addition, its wells and refineries supplied oil for the Allied military operations in that part of the world. It is quite evident, however, that United States' interest and financial support went far beyond the requirements of the wartime emergency. Nor can it be said that the millions of dollars which the United States spent in aid to this country was oc-

7. *New York Times*, February 8, 1946.

casioned merely by a desire to support a large and productive American investment. Arabian oil is an important link in the foreign oil policy of the United States Government, however vague and shifting that policy may be. The extent of United States' interest may be understood in part by the fact that during the latter part of the war the United States was seriously considering the direct purchase of all or a part of the oil producing facilities of American companies in the area. This development will be dealt with in the next chapter.

Before the war the most important source of foreign exchange and revenue of the Saudi Arabian Government was the annual pilgrimage to the Holy Cities. Some 80,000-100,000 pilgrims from all over the Moslem world brought in an estimated $5 to $6 million in gold sovereigns and foreign exchange, the bulk of which accrued to the Saudi Arabian Government in the form of fees and payments for local transportation. During the war this traffic was cut from one-half to two-thirds with a consequent reduction in revenues.[8] Since Saudi Arabia depends for a substantial proportion of its food, textiles, and other necessities upon imports from abroad, the population was threatened with starvation in the absence of outside assistance. The political stability of the country was also in jeopardy since the King depends upon liberal subsidies of money and commodities to the tribes for support in maintaining order in the country. In order to assure political stability and loyalty among the Arab countries and to avoid interference with her lines of communication, Britain began granting financial assistance to Saudi Arabia in the form of commodities and gold early in the war. In 1943 the United States added Saudi Arabia to the list of countries entitled to lend-lease assistance and beginning with 1944 cooperated with Britain in a program of aid on a fifty-fifty basis. It should be pointed out, however, that total assistance to Saudi

8. During 1944 revenues from the pilgrimage were estimated to be 10.3 million riyals or about 3.1 million dollars. The real value of this revenue was of course further reduced by the rise in the prices of imports.

Arabia, including about $10 million in loans by the Arabian-American Oil Company, was several times the annual loss on pilgrimage revenues.

Our initial aid to Saudi Arabia took the form of silver supplied out of United States Treasury stocks under a special lend-lease contract, the silver to be minted into riyal coins.[9] Both the Saudi Arabian Government and the oil company were embarrassed in 1943 by a shortage of silver riyals, the standard money of the realm.[10] The high price of silver in India and the surrounding countries caused the silver coins to be exported or withdrawn from circulation by native hoarders. Riyals had to be purchased by the Oil Company and the government for meeting payrolls and other local expenditures with gold sovereigns, the value of which was also quite high in the Middle East during the war.[11] An added complication arose out of the fact that the pilgrims had to buy riyals to meet their personal expenses during their visit to the Holy Cities. In order to keep down the cost of the pilgrimage the Saudi Arabian Government undertook to guarantee a minimum rate of 40 riyals to the sovereign during the periods of the annual pilgrimage in 1943 and 1944. The government was aided in this effort by the timely arrival in the fall of 1943 of a substantial shipment of riyals from the United States. Later on additional riyals were supplied under the lend-lease arrangement mentioned above, a portion of which was sold to the oil company and to the American Legation in Jidda.[12]

9. During the period 1943-1945, 22.3 million ounces of silver were lend-leased to Saudi Arabia. According to the lend-lease contract the silver must be returned to the Treasury within five years after the end of the war emergency period. *Annual Report of the Secretary of the Treasury for Fiscal Year Ended June 30, 1944*, pp. 86-87.

10. The Saudi Arabian riyal has a silver content of 180 grains, eleven-twelfths fine. The official foreign exchange value is 1s 6d or $.30 United States.

11. Sovereigns were quoted at from $16 to $20 apiece in terms of Middle East currencies during the war. The value of the gold contained in the sovereign at $35 per ounce is $8.24.

12. For a more complete discussion of Saudi Arabia's currency problems see R. F. Mikesell, "Monetary Developments in Saudi Arabia," *The Middle East Journal*, April, 1947.

When lend-lease riyals were sold to the oil company or to the Legation, the Saudi Arabian Government was required to deposit 60 per cent of the dollar proceeds in a special reserve fund for the eventual repurchase of the silver for return to the United States Treasury. Within the next five years Saudi Arabia should have sufficient dollar resources from royalties to repurchase all of the silver which she is required to return to the United States.

In addition to the silver Saudi Arabia received over 17.5 million dollars worth of lend-lease supplies from this country, largely in the form of essential civilian goods. A United States Agricultural Mission and a United States Military Mission were also sent to assist the country. American and British financial assistance, together with substantial loans by the oil company, have enabled the country to meet its large budgetary deficits, running from $10 to $15 million annually, until oil royalties increase to the point where it can stand on its own feet economically. With oil royalties now running at an estimated $30 million annually, and with good prospects of their being doubled in the next five years, Saudi Arabia should not require any further financial assistance other than long-term development loans in amounts which she is financially able to service.[18]

The Saudi Arabian Government has a number of postwar projects, principally in the field of communications. Two of these projects, the development of a port at Dammam near the center of Aramco's oil production on the Persian Gulf and a 350-mile railway from Dammam to Riyadh, are already in the initial stages. Aramco is reported to have agreed to lend the government $40 million for these two projects against future oil royalties. The government is also seeking an Export-Import Bank loan of $20 to $25 million for a railroad linking Jidda on the Red Sea coast with the holy cities, Mecca

13. To complete the picture of United States financial aid to Saudi Arabia mention should be made of a $2 million credit for the purchase of United States surplus war materials and a $10 million Export-Import Bank loan in 1946.

and Medina. Before World War I a railroad operated between Damascus and Medina, largely for carrying the pilgrim traffic, but the southern portion of the line was destroyed in the course of the Allied operations against the Turks. Ibn Saud hopes eventually to reconstruct the destroyed portion of this line, reestablishing direct rail communication with Maan in Transjordan, the present terminus of the railroad to Damascus. Finally the King hopes to establish another railroad which would connect Riyadh and the Persian Gulf coast to the west coast and the proposed line to Medina. Although the King has a marked affinity for railroads, many engineers are of the opinion that a network of highways would be much more economical and would better serve Arabia's communication requirements.

In a recent public statement, Saudi Arabia's Minister of Development, Fuad Bey Hamza, outlined a series of capital development projects requiring a total outlay of $270 million. In addition to those mentioned above, the project includes 1200 miles of highways, airfields at Riyadh, Mecca, and other cities, the electrification of the major cities, and the construction of city water systems. The Minister of Development expects to be able to finance these projects largely from oil royalties, or loans secured by royalties which he anticipates will achieve a level of $50 million annually in the early 1950's.[14]

GOVERNMENT RELATIONS WITH THE OIL COMPANY

The relations between company officials and the Saudi Arabian Government appear to be quite harmonious and the extent of their cooperation provides a unique chapter in the history of foreign investment.[15] The confidence which

---

14. For a report of Fuad Bey Hamza's statement, see *The New York Times*, July 18, 1947, p. 1.

15. According to the information of the authors, there has been only one serious dispute between the government and the oil company. This controversy concerns the interpretation of the method of

the company enjoys with the government is due in part to the non-political interest of the company in its internal affairs, a factor which must be taken into consideration in any projected schemes for United States Government participation in operating the concessions. However, until recently the King has been much more favorably disposed toward the American Government [16] than toward the British because he believes that the former has less political interest in his internal affairs. Although Ibn Saud's relations with the British are friendly he is anxious to avoid any political entanglements which would jeopardize his sovereignty.

In all of Saudi Arabia's relations with the United States Government the Arabian American Oil Company has played a major role. Company officials frequently serve as informal advisers to the King and his ministers and perform the function of an unofficial ambassador in Washington, where the company maintains an office. This type of relationship, although admittedly subject to abuse, appears to have been quite advantageous for a government which until the last few years has had little diplomatic or economic contact with the outside world. Moreover, so long as the foreign oil policy of the United States coincides more or less with that of the oil company, the arrangement may continue to be useful to the United States Government.

The long range policy of the Oil Company has been to promote the economic welfare and education of the Arab community. This program has been undertaken not only for the obvious purpose of building up good will with the public and the government, but also as a means of developing a supply of capable personnel for its operations. It is not enough for the company simply to train workers and to pay good wages. An Arab cannot suddenly be thrust into a job paying

---

royalty payments under the terms of the concession contract. (See Chapter IX for a discussion of this controversy.)

16. The only source of irritation between Ibn Saud and the United States Government has been American sponsorship of Jewish immigration into Palestine and its partition into a Jewish and an Arab state.

more money per week than he ordinarily may have seen in a whole year and then be sent home at night to his tent in the desert or to a mud house in his primitive oasis village. The worker must be sociologically conditioned to a different mode of living if he is not to be spoiled in the process. It is also a fact that one of the most important contributions to productivity which flows from a higher standard of living lies in the improved health of the worker. Contrary to popular impression, Arabs are not especially healthy but have a very high disease rate, particularly in large communities where the most ordinary sanitation facilities do not exist. Therefore it is essential from the standpoint of the effectiveness of the worker that his increased money income provide the physical conditions of healthful living for himself and his family.

In order to improve the living standards and productivity of the workers in the refineries and oil fields, the oil company has built whole towns near its operations where no settlements have existed before. In addition to modern homes of different sizes depending upon the income and the needs of the native workers, the company has provided schools, hospital, and medical centers for the communities.[17] The new Arabian towns of Dammam, Ras Tanura, Dhahran, and Manama hold a large part of the company's 15,000 native workers as well as the 5,000 American and 1300 Italian employees. These towns are probably destined to become great Arabian cities in the future, especially as commercial and manufacturing enterprises are established in these centers. The company is anxious for both native and foreign enterprises of various kinds to locate in these towns in order to provide a more balanced economy. There is also an opportunity for industries based upon the utilization of refinery by-products.

While the advantages of working for the company are

---

17. This practice is also followed in other Middle East oil-producing countries. For example, the city of Abadan which is the site of the Anglo-Iranian Oil Company's principal refinery was built in large part by the oil company. Its population is nearly 200,000.

obvious for thousands of impoverished Arabs who have never had steady jobs in their lives, these benefits can reach only a small percentage of the country's estimated population of 4.5 million. Of greater importance to the rest of the country is the extra-contractual aid which the company has been able to provide Ibn Saud in the way of technical assistance. Mention has already been made of the possibility of increasing the agricultural potential of Arabia. To this end the company has drilled a number of water wells and also has converted abandoned test oil wells to water wells whenever possible. In 1941 the Saudi Government appealed to the company for engineering assistance in connection with an irrigation project at Al Kharj south of Riyadh. Two years later company engineers took over complete supervision of this work with the government supplying the labor. Lend-lease funds and U. S. Department of Agriculture experts were also made available for an agricultural project by the United States Government. As a result of the installation of modern pumping equipment in an old oasis and the construction of an eleven mile canal, 2,000 acres of additional land have already been placed under cultivation.[18] Other technical aid has included the installation of wireless facilities, the maintenance of automotive equipment, building roads, and experimentation in scientific agricultural methods.

THE NEED FOR ECONOMIC REFORM

The ultimate benefits of the oil operations to Saudi Arabia and to the other oil producing areas of the Middle East must be measured in terms of their effects on the well-being of the common people. Whether or not the royalty payments and local expenditures of the oil companies are to make a significant contribution to the economic and social welfare of the nearly 30 million Arabs living in the Persian Gulf area will depend on the way these funds are employed. On the basis of rates of production in late 1947 royalty payments by oil

18. *Petroleum Interests in Foreign Countries*, pp. 286-87. See also Fanning, *American Oil Operations Abroad*, pp. 194 ff.

companies in Persian Gulf countries are in excess of $60 million annually. In Saudi Arabia royalty payments are running at about $21 million per year with an additional $5 million in local payroll expenditures. A company official has forecast that by 1952 production of crude oil will be at the rate of 700,000 barrels per day which will mean royalty payments in excess of $50 million annually plus additional local expenditures of perhaps $10 million annually. Although these are substantial sums, they will represent per capita payments of less than $15 per year. The significance of these payments, however, is not in their direct contribution to the per capita income of the country, but in the fact that they represent foreign exchange income which can be utilized for the industrial and agricultural development of the Arab countries. If these sums, plus what can properly be borrowed against future income, are spent on scientific agricultural development, industrialization, communications, and educational, health, and other social services, it may be possible to bring the living standard of the Arabs up to a level approaching that of Western countries within a generation. On the other hand, if the oil royalties are used principally for the importation of private motor cars and other luxuries by a few wealthy merchants, government officials and landowners, and if the wages of the oil company employees are spent on commodities from abroad which ought to be produced locally, the newly discovered wealth will contribute little to the economic well-being of the vast bulk of the people of the Middle East.

If Saudi Arabia's newly discovered wealth is to be utilized for the economic progress and the social welfare of the nation as a whole, certain modern institutions and administrative machinery will have to be adopted. Among these should be included an efficient currency and foreign exchange system, modern banking facilities, an adequate fiscal system and tax administration, import and export controls, and a comprehensive long-range economic program for the country. Mention has already been made of the fact that both the government and private interests, including the foreign companies, have frequently been embarrassed by the lack of adequate supplies of riyals. It is an important function of government to supply sufficient currency to meet the needs of industry and trade, no matter how primitive the economy may be. The continued dependence on foreign coins and silver riyals whose bullion value has a tendency to fluctuate widely in world markets makes it impossible for the Saudi Arabian Government to adequately discharge this function.[19] The future development of industry and trade in Saudi Arabia will depend in considerable measure upon the institution of an appropriate monetary mechanism.

Much the same may be said regarding the need for a banking system. There are only two banking institutions in Saudi Arabia: the Netherlands Trading Society and Gellatly Hantey & Co., Ltd., both of which are located in Jidda.[20] These concerns perform various services for foreign traders including the purchase and sale of foreign exchange and currencies. Their activities are supplemented by hundreds of money-changers who profit by the chaotic currency situation in the country. A banking system worthy of the name is needed to provide credit facilities on reasonable terms and other financial assistance to the business and agricultural community. A modern bank would also provide a savings medium and a source of capital for private and governmental enterprises. At present merchants and others with surplus funds tend to invest their wealth in land or accumulate hoards of coin or precious metals, neither of which contributes to the productivity of the economy.

19. Saudi Arabia has no paper currency. Although the silver riyal is the official medium of exchange the *de facto* monetary standard is the English gold sovereign which is used widely by both the government and private interests as a means of payment. For specific suggestions on monetary reforms in Saudi Arabia, see R. F. Mikesell, "Monetary Problems of Saudi Arabia," *The Middle East Journal*, April, 1947.

20. In the summer of 1948 a branch of the Banque l'Indo-Chine was established at Jidda. The bank will perform certain monetary functions for the government.

The government is also greatly in need of a bank to serve as its fiscal agent and to handle its foreign exchange transactions. A banking system is essential to the proper channeling of the foreign exchange which the government receives from foreign concessions, the pilgrimage, and other sources. Foreign exchange over and above what the government needs for its own purposes should be sold at fixed prices to merchants for the importation of essential commodities. Foreign exchange controls and a system of import licensing should be instituted in order to assure that the foreign exchange resources of the country are employed in the most productive manner. Such controls should operate in close cooperation with an industrial and agricultural planning body whose function would be to secure the coordination of government and private enterprise in a long range development program.

It should not be inferred that we are suggesting a thoroughgoing system of governmental controls for Saudi Arabia. Actually private traders play a relatively minor role in Saudi Arabia's foreign trade at the present time and we believe that a large part of the foreign buying which is now done by the government should be transferred to private hands. However, it is generally recognized that in undeveloped countries where the bulk of the wealth is in the hands of landowners, governmental initiative and guidance are essential for rapid economic progress.

Economic progress and social welfare also require an efficient fiscal system. Western budgetary and fiscal practices are almost unknown in Saudi Arabia. The bulk of the government's revenue comes from the pilgrimage and from the royalties paid by the Arabian-American Oil Company and the Mining Syndicate. Tax receipts, which account for only about 5 per cent of total revenues, are derived largely from customs duties and the *ushr*, a 10 per cent levy on all produce payable in kind.[21] Tax administration, which is based on the Ottoman system of farming out the collection of

21. There is in addition a head tax on all persons not subject to the *ushr* and who are not serving in the army.

taxes, is grossly inefficient and subject to widespread abuses. Extensive smuggling also reduces the yield from customs duties.

Perhaps even more significant is the method of expenditure of public revenues. Since the bulk of the revenue from the oil operations is paid directly to the government, a substantial portion of the government's income is used to pay subsidies to the tribes either in the form of money or in the form of commodities imported for that purpose. Since there is little distinction between the revenues of the monarch and those of the state which he governs, the payments appear as the largess of a benevolent tribal leader to his less opulent followers. Not only does such a system involve injustices, no matter how good the intentions of the despot may be, but it stifles initiative and productivity in the community. It would not be possible to cut off subsidies immediately since many tribesmen cannot produce enough to keep themselves alive. But the subsidy funds should be used to provide productive employment and to rehabilitate tribes which are not self-sufficient in their present abodes.

The oil companies operating in the Middle East and the foreign governments which they represent have a measure of responsibility in using their influence to see that the oil revenues are properly channeled. Such a policy need not involve forcing the local governments to commit themselves to a program of economic and social reform under the threat of economic and political sanctions. These countries cannot be driven into economic and political democracy; they must be led into, and convinced of the advantages of, liberal democratic culture at its best. Nor should a frontal attack be made on the deeply rooted traditions of the Moslem peoples in an obvious attempt to "westernize" the area. Many of the laws and customs such as, for example, polygamy are based on the teachings of the Koran, and a direct attack on Koranic law would be met with widespread resentment. But the Koran, like the Bible, is a flexible instrument and its passages are sufficiently vague to permit a variety of interpretations. Given a program of education and economic opportunities for the masses of Arabs, the customs of the past may take on less objectionable forms.

The realization of these objectives in countries with virtually no educated liberal class will require the greatest tact and diplomacy. Much could probably be done in Saudi Arabia with the aid of American economic and social advisors if the King were willing to accept them. Since Ibn Saud has on many occasions shown himself to be progressively minded, it should not be too difficult for the oil company and the United States State Department to convince him of the desirability of obtaining American technical assistance. The appointment of technical advisors and the establishment of certain economic reforms can often be properly included under the terms of a loan. Much can also be done by means of informal advice by diplomatic officials and the representatives of the oil company. Relatively small sums spent in the form of grants-in-aid for welfare purposes can often be accompanied by a program which is later sustained and developed by the local government once the government is convinced of its merit and its popularity with the people.

The economic and social structure of the Arab states presents many obstacles to reform. The landowning aristocracy is largely indifferent to industrialization or to change of any kind, and the fellahin are too abysmally ignorant and wretched to be counted on to take any initiative whatsoever. Such democratic institutions as exist in countries like Egypt and Iraq are rather superficial. Election campaigns are not concerned for the most part with social issues, but consist largely of swaying the masses of voters with nationalistic slogans, bribes, and empty promises. Saudi Arabia lacks even these outward trimmings of political democracy, nor would it be especially helpful to establish them in the immediate future. There must be an educational and economic basis for political democracy; otherwise popular elections become the medium through which dictators of either the right or the left may arise. Moreover democracy must begin with local government. If local government is autocratic, popular elections of national representatives become a sham.

For the time being, and until the social conditions for democracy can be developed, reforms in Saudi Arabia (and perhaps elsewhere in the Middle East) must be imposed from above. Although Ibn Saud is one of the most absolute monarchs in the world, he appears to use his power largely for the benefit of his people. It is to the King or perhaps to his successor, Crown Prince Saud, that we must look to overcome the opposition of the landed aristocracy and wealthy merchants to fundamental economic and political reforms. The King has made remarkable progress in converting the warlike tribesmen to the ways of peace and in persuading the Bedouin tribes to settle down in agricultural communities. Travel is now safe over most of Arabia. The King is actively interested in the promotion of scientific farming, the improvement of communications, and the construction of public works. But the King, whose power was built on the loyalty of fanatic Wahabbi [22] tribesmen, must proceed slowly in dealing with the traditional customs and prejudices of the tribes.[23]

22. The Wahabbi religion is based on a literal interpretation of the Koran and the strictest adherence to the Moslem code. The Wahabbis are the puritans among the Moslems.
23. For example it was necessary for the King to have certain passages of the Koran read over the government's broadcasting station in order to convince the religious leaders that the radio was not an instrument of the devil.

CHAPTER VII

MIDDLE EAST OIL AND UNITED STATES FOREIGN POLICY

THE DETERMINATION OF United States Government policy with regard to a strategic material involves a conflict between two established American principles: conservation to assure self-sufficiency in time of emergency, and the maintenance of competitive private enterprise and free trade. This fundamental dichotomy, which pervades most of the debates on our foreign economic policy, lies at the heart of the complex struggle for the development of a foreign oil policy in the United States during the past five years. A democratic capitalistic society will endure so long as it is able to find, within the framework of that society, a satisfactory solution to the problems which the international economic and political environment present. The petroleum problem is one of many which today present this challenge. But before attempting to arrive at any conclusions, we will review the recent actions and policies of the United States Government with respect to American petroleum interests abroad. It will be seen that for the most part these actions were concerned with our interests in the Middle East.

THE PETROLEUM RESERVES CORPORATION

In July 1943 there was created by Executive Order the Petroleum Reserves Corporation whose charter gave it broad powers to acquire reserves of crude petroleum from sources outside the United States and to construct and operate refineries, pipe lines, and other facilities abroad.[1] The President of the PRC was the Secretary of the Interior (and Petroleum

1. *The Federal Register*, July 2, 1943, p. 9044. See Appendix.

Administrator for War) and its Board of Directors included the Secretaries of State, War, and Navy and the head of the Foreign Economic Administration. From the events which followed it became evident that the immediate purpose of the PRC was the acquisition of privately held American oil concessions in the Middle East. The details of the intra-governmental debates which preceded the determination of this important policy decision will not concern us here,[2] but the attempts to implement this policy form a significant chapter in the history of American participation in Middle East oil.

In July 1943 President Roosevelt authorized the PRC to negotiate for the purchase of the stock of the Arabian-American Oil Company and the Bahrein Petroleum Company.[3] Previous to this decision the owners of these two companies had offered the United States Government an option to buy a portion of the underground oil reserves in Saudi Arabia under concession to the Arabian-American Oil Company. The Secretary of the Interior and the heads of certain other government departments, however, thought that such an arrangement would not provide the government with a sufficient stake in these oil reserves to justify in the eyes of Congress and the public their complete protection to the full extent of our diplomatic and military power. Moreover, the United States Government would not be able to control the rate of production of the reserves of the entire concession nor the conditions of marketing. It was therefore decided to negotiate for outright purchase of the concessions and the existing oil facilities. After protracted discussion during

---

2. For an account of these discussions see Herbert Feis, *Seen from E. A.* (New York: Alfred A. Knopf, 1947). According to Mr. Feis the responsibility for this decision was largely that of Secretary of the Interior Ickes, with the active support of the Secretaries of War and Navy. Throughout the subsequent negotiations the State Department evidently entertained serious doubts as to the advisability of the direct acquisition of foreign concessions. See also *A History of the Petroleum Administration for War*, U. S. Government Printing Office, Washington, 1946, pp. 276-79.

3. Feis, *op. cit.*, p. 122.

which the proposal was amended to provide for the purchase of only a minority interest in the concessions, the Standard of California and Texas Companies announced their refusal to sell.[4] The reasons for this refusal on the part of the companies are quite understandable. They had invested millions of dollars on a gamble that now had good prospects of paying off far beyond their most optimistic expectations. The government would probably not have paid them much more than the costs which had been incurred in developing the concession, while they had borne all of the risks. They wanted government support in any future conflicts which they might have with the local government or with third powers, and they had hoped to obtain this support by granting an option to the government covering a portion of the reserves. But to sell the entire concession was like throwing away the baby with the bath water. Moreover, the intense interest of the government in American oil production in the Middle East indicated that the companies might be able to count on the full support of the United States Government without giving up any of their investment. Finally, the companies were opposed in principle to government ownership and competition for fear of repercussions on their operations in other parts of the world.[5]

Following the failure of these efforts for outright purchase, the government adopted a new tactic. On February 6, 1944, the President of the Petroleum Reserves Corporation, Secretary Ickes, announced a tentative agreement with the presidents of the Arabian-American Oil Company and the Gulf Exploration Company [6] whereby the Petroleum Reserves Corporation would construct and operate a pipe line which would convey the oil from the Saudi Arabian and Kuwait oil

4. *Ibid.*, Chapter VII. Discussions were also carried on by the government with the Gulf Oil Company for the purchase of its half interest in the Kuwait Concession.

5. Herbert Feis, *Petroleum and American Foreign Policy*, Food Research Institute, Stanford University, California, pp. 38-39.

6. The Gulf Exploration Company, a subsidiary of the Gulf Oil Corporation, owns half interest in the Kuwait Petroleum Company.

fields to a port on the eastern Mediterranean.⁷ In addition to the pipe-line system the other principal features of the contemplated agreement were as follows:

(1) A crude-oil reserve of 1 billion barrels, or 20 per cent of the total crude reserves held by the companies if these reserves prove to be less than 5 billion barrels, was to be maintained for the account of the military forces of the United States Government.

(2) The United States Government was to have the option to purchase the reserved oil at a discount of 25 per cent below the market price.

(3) The charges for the pipe line service by the Petroleum Reserves Corporation were to be sufficient to cover maintenance and operating costs and, in addition, to amortize the entire investment within a period of 25 years, together with interest and an agreed net return.

(4) The companies were to give prior notice to the State Department of negotiations with the governments of any foreign countries relating to the sale of products from their concessions in Saudi Arabia and Kuwait.

(5) No sales of petroleum by the companies were to be made to any government or its nationals if, in the opinion of the State Department, such sales would militate against the interests of the United States. The commercial and other policies and practices of the companies were to conform to the foreign policy of the United States Government.

It is clear that the purpose of the proposed agreement was not simply to provide a government oil reserve and to facilitate its transportation by means of a pipe line. A more significant purpose was to assure that all of the oil produced by American concerns in these two concessions would be sold in conformity with United States foreign policy.⁸ The proved

---

7. The text of Mr. Ickes' announcement was printed in the *Congressional Record*, Senate Proceedings, February 9, 1944, pp. 1468 ff. See Appendix for the text of the announcement.

8. The agreement did not of course cover the sale of oil by the Anglo-Iranian Oil Company, Gulf's partner in the Kuwait concession.

reserves of the Arabian-American Oil Company, plus Gulf's share in the reserves of the Kuwait concession total 11½ billion barrels, an amount equal to nearly half the proved reserves in continental United States. It was also believed that government ownership of the pipe line would secure more complete protection of the American concessions in Saudi Arabia and Kuwait.[9]

The proposed agreement met with a storm of protest from the oil industry as a whole and a cool reception in Congress. The Petroleum Industry War Council condemned the agreement as unnecessary and harmful to the interests of the United States in protecting our oil position, unfair to domestic and other foreign producers, and a violation of the principles of the Atlantic Charter.[10] It was attacked as an unwarranted intrusion by the government in a field in which American private enterprise and initiative have made remarkable progress. Concern over government competition was expressed by American companies operating in South America, whose European markets might be affected by the arrangement, and by other American companies holding an interest in concessions in the Middle East.

It is possible that some of the opposition to the contemplated agreement might have been avoided by prior consultation with the oil industry. Apparently neither American interests nor the foreign governments immediately concerned were consulted.[11] Although the agreement did not require congressional action it was obviously unwise to go through with it in the face of growing opposition in Congress. In

9. Secretary of the Navy Knox, in his testimony on the Naval Appropriations Bill for 1945 made the following statement on the pipe line proposal: "It protected American ownership in these tremendous concessions; that was a major factor, because we assumed, and I trust it is a correct assumption, if the United States Government was vitally interested in this field, no one is going to come there or take the concession away."

10. *United States Foreign Oil Policy and Petroleum Reserves Corporation*, Petroleum Industry War Council, Washington, D. C., March, 1944.

11. See Feis, *Seen From E. A.*, p. 140.

June 1944 the President therefore agreed to take no further action on the matter without notifying the Senate, and the proposal was put aside pending an investigation by a special Senate committee. The failure of the two proposals for direct participation on the part of the government in Middle East oil operations opened the way for an attempt to realize our general foreign oil objectives by means of an international agreement.

THE ANGLO-AMERICAN OIL AGREEMENT

Although the idea of an international oil agreement had been simmering in the State Department since the spring of 1943,[12] action on an agreement with Britain was not taken until after the failure of the government pipe-line construction plan. The first Anglo-American Petroleum Agreement was signed on August 8, 1944. Although they are not specifically mentioned, the agreement was devised principally to deal with the common problems of the two nations in the Middle East. The fundamental purposes of the agreement may be summarized as follows:

(1) To establish the principle of equal opportunity in the acquisition of concessions. Specifically this meant that neither country would seek to prevent by diplomatic means the acquisition of concessions by the nationals of the other country, and each country would refrain from interfering with existing valid contracts held by the nationals of the other country.

(2) To establish the principle of equal access in the distribution of petroleum and petroleum products. Subject to considerations of military security, it was agreed that the government and the nationals of each country would make oil available on a fair and non-discriminatory basis to all countries.

(3) To establish a mechanism for dealing with disputes which might arise between the two countries in connection with the production of petroleum and to provide for continu-

12. *Ibid.*, Chapter VIII.

ous study and consultation on problems of joint interest. To accomplish these and other purposes the agreement provided for a joint International Petroleum Commission with power to make recommendations tò the two governments.

Although the agreement appears to be innocuous enough, the already suspicious and sensitive oil industry misconstrued its meaning and intent. The terms of the agreement which dealt with the distribution of petroleum products on a fair and non-discriminatory basis were believed to mean that the United States Government would be given complete authority to regulate the international sale of petroleum. The industry took the view that the government was seeking to accomplish by international agreement what it failed to achieve in the proposed concession purchase and pipe-line deals. Fears were also expressed that the agreement might impair the right of the United States to regulate imports into this country; that the agreement gave the federal government power to regulate domestic production and distribution; and that it encroached upon the rights of the states to control the production of petroleum within their borders. In fairness to the critics it is generally agreed that the proposed agreement was extremely vague and difficult to understand.

The proposed agreement was presented to Congress in the fall of 1944 but was later withdrawn by the President from the Senate Foreign Relations Committee in the face of strong opposition. After extended consultation with the industry a new text was drafted which appeared to have a larger measure of support among the representatives of the industry. The amended Anglo-American Oil Agreement was signed by American and British government representatives on September 24, 1945. The broad purposes of the new agreement are the same as before. The industry was assured that nothing in the agreement was to be construed as requiring compliance on the part of the governments or the companies to the recommendations of the International Petroleum Commission, whether or not those recommendations were approved by the governments. The document also states that the agreement in no way affects the right of either government to control imports.¹³

The new Anglo-American Agreement was transmitted to the Senate on November 1, 1945, but hearings before the Committee on Foreign Relations did not begin until June 2, 1947.¹⁴ After several weeks of hearings the agreement was reported favorably with two minor amendments and certain reservations on July 7, 1947, but there is likely to be formidable opposition when and if it reaches the Senate floor.¹⁵ Nevertheless, it is worth while reviewing a few of its salient features with reference to the special problems of Middle East oil. The principal value of the agreement is to forestall any conflicts between the British and the American governments over the acquisition of new concessions and any interference by either government with valid concessions contracts held by nationals of the other government. Since conflicts between the oil companies inevitably involve their respective governments, the provisions of the agreement dealing with the acquisition of exploration and development rights have considerable significance.

The principle of "equal opportunity" in the acquisition of oil rights, stated in Article II of the agreement, is difficult to apply in practice. It may only mean that one government will not bar, by political or economic measures, the acquisition by nationals of other countries of concession rights in its own territory or in the territory of third countries. It may also mean that the signatory governments will discourage the acquisition of large and exclusive concessions which effectively prohibit the entry of competitors in an oil producing

13. The text of the amended Anglo-American Petroleum Agreement and the Senate Foreign Relations Committee's amendments and reservations are given in the Appendix.

14. See *Hearings*, Senate Committee on Foreign Relations, Eightieth Congress, First Session, on Executive H, June 2-25, 1947; see also, *Report of Senate Committee on Foreign Relations, Anglo-American Oil Agreement*, Eightieth Congress, First Session, July 7, 1947.

15. The Committee voted 11 to 1 for approval with Senator Connolly of Texas opposing. At the time of writing it appears doubtful whether the proposed agreement will ever be acted on by the Senate.

country.[16] The tendency for concession contracts to cover all of the territory of a country favorable to oil discovery has already caused the bulk of the world's petroleum reserves to be monopolized by a few large concerns and, if continued, will effectually shut out all future competition for concessions.[17] The present tendency in the Middle East is to divide up concessions among the nationals of two or more countries by the formation of a new concessionaire company whose stock is owned by two or more major companies. This is the situation, for example, in Iraq, Kuwait, and Qatar. Where the nationals of one country hold the only concession, as in the case of Iran, arrangements have been made for the sharing of the product between British and American interests through output sharing agreements and the joint ownership of pipe lines. This tendency is exemplified by the recent agreement between Anglo-Iranian and the Jersey-Socony interests for the sharing of the output of Iran. The same companies which have been permitted to share in the ownership or the output of the exclusive concessions are themselves holders of important concessions in the Middle East and elsewhere. The new agreements do nothing to advance the principles of equal opportunity for exploration and a fair sharing of the product with respect to the nationals of other countries or to other competing American and British companies.[18] As has already been noted, prac-

[16]. Recently the State Department asked an American company which was negotiating for a nation-wide exclusive concession in Paraguay to restrict the area for which the concession was sought in order to leave room for competitive companies.

[17]. The Sinclair Oil Corporation in 1944 obtained a concession from the Ethiopian Government covering 350,000 square miles, the entire area of the country.

[18]. In August 1947 a group of eleven United States companies joined together to form the American Independent Oil Company to engage in foreign petroleum operations "particularly in the Middle East." This action is reported to have been encouraged by the State Department which is interested not only in strengthening the American oil position in the Middle East but also in securing a wider distribution of ownership among American companies.—*Wall Street Journal*, August 2, 1947; see also *New York Times*, August 20, 1947.

tically all of the Persian Gulf area with the exception of Yemen (about whose oil possibilities little is known) and the Sheikh of Kuwait's half interest in the Neutral Zone is already under exclusive concession.

The International Petroleum Commission provided for in Article IV of the Anglo-American Oil Agreement would be particularly valuable under present conditions of a worldwide shortage of oil and the probable shift in the pattern of trade over the next four years. The commission would have only advisory functions and neither signatory government has any obligation under the terms of the proposed agreement to comply with its recommendations. Moreover, similar international commissions have been established for a number of other internationally traded commodities. Yet opponents of the agreement maintain that the establishment of the International Petroleum Commission would involve the creation of a world-wide petroleum cartel and federal regulation of domestic and international petroleum production and trade under international agreement. The Senate Foreign Affairs Committee took pains to clarify each clause of the agreement to remove every reasonable doubt as to its meaning. The opposition on the part of a large section of the American petroleum industry must therefore be found not in the letter of the agreement, but in its broader implications.[19] It is quite conceivable that an International Petroleum Commission might recommend the world-wide allocation of petroleum to meet a specific situation or they might recommend production controls in certain areas. Those who oppose governmental controls under any circumstances are led to condemn the establishment of a commission even for the purpose of studying world petroleum problems, for fear that this might

19. Witnesses testifying in favor of the agreement included Eugene Holman, President of the Standard Oil Company (N. J.), and W. R. Boyd, President of the American Petroleum Institute. Opponents included R. B. Brown, Independent Petroleum Associations of America, Henry S. Fraser on behalf of the Sinclair Oil Co., and H. J. Porter, President of the Texas Independent Producers and Royalty Owners Association.

be a first step in the direction of federal and international control. This is a short-sighted policy even for those who do not like controls. For when the vital interests of the public demand the institution of controls, they will be imposed with or without an international advisory commission. Meanwhile it is better that we do not bury our heads in the sand and deal with our problems only after they have reached a crisis stage, if appropriate steps can be taken on a voluntary basis now.

A MULTILATERAL PETROLEUM AGREEMENT

According to the preamble of the Anglo-American Petroleum Agreement, this bilateral agreement is only a preliminary measure to the calling of an international conference for the negotiation of a multilateral petroleum agreement.[20] In such a conference the interests of the consumers and the oil producing countries, as well as the producing companies and their governments, should be adequately represented. The following questions have been suggested as ones with which a United Nations conference might deal:

(1) access on equal terms to petroleum and petroleum products by all countries;

(2) greater opportunity on the part of countries without oil resources to obtain concessions in the unassigned areas of the world favorable to oil discovery;

(3) provisions in concession contracts to protect the welfare of the countries in which oil is produced;

(4) measures for the economic development of backward oil producing countries;

(5) the proper utilization of the world's oil resources;

(6) trade and foreign exchange restrictions affecting the marketing of petroleum; and

(7) the avoidance of harmful and restrictive practices on the part of the oil companies.

20. In a radio broadcast on the NBC University of the Air Series on August 17, 1946, Mr. John H. Loftus, then Chief of Petroleum Division, Department of State, suggested that such a conference might be called by the United Nations Economic and Social Council.

We will deal briefly with certain aspects of these questions with reference to the special problems of the Middle East.

Unless a deliberate effort were made to break up the existing exclusive concessions in the Middle East, it may be too late to talk about independents getting into Middle East production on a large scale. Not only are unassigned areas of future production limited, but there are serious marketing difficulties for new firms. Marketing outlets in the Eastern Hemisphere are controlled by a few American, British, French, and Dutch firms. Governmental interferences and exchange restrictions present obstacles to the entry of new competitors which do not exist in the United States. Moreover, European countries are seeking to build their own refineries to save foreign exchange, and there is a general trend toward the nationalization of all industries, including petroleum production and distribution. Shipping Middle East petroleum to American markets, however, may become feasible on a substantial scale once the new pipe lines to the Mediterranean are completed and the tanker shortage has been eased.

Turning to the question of a fair distribution of petroleum products among all consuming countries and the avoidance of harmful monopolistic practices, an international convention dealing with these problems has much to offer. So long as petroleum is not in short supply in the world—and it appears that by 1955 supplies will probably be sufficient to meet peacetime demands the world over—it should not be difficult to enforce the rule of nondiscrimination in regard to terms and conditions of sale. American companies have usually been willing to follow this rule voluntarily; if not, means should be found to require them to do so. Far more difficult in applying the principle of equal access on the part of all consuming countries is the foreign exchange problem. For example, when American companies demand dollars for the oil which they produce, it represents a drain on the foreign exchange resources of countries whose gold and dollar resources are severely limited. Some relief might be afforded by a conscious effort on the part of the companies operating abroad to expand their purchases of supplies from the countries to whom their oil is sold, but profits and amortization payments to American investors must be paid in dollars. In the final analysis this becomes a part of the basic problem of the balance of payments of the United States, the solution of which depends upon the supply of dollars which we make available to the rest of the world through our imports of commodities and services and through our foreign loans and direct investments.

Mention was made of the fact that the proposed Charter for an International Trade Organization outlaws all private commercial agreements involving the fixing of prices, of marketing, and of production quotas. Such a blanket prohibition is scarcely applicable to the oil cartel problem in the Middle East. Middle East oil production and marketing is in the hands of a tight oligopoly, and the technical and organizational conditions for competition simply do not exist. Because of the non-competitive nature of the markets of the Eastern Hemisphere in which the product is sold, agreements for sharing the product and uniform pricing policies are inevitable.[21] The ITO Charter does provide, however, for intergovernmental commodity control agreements covering the production, marketing, and pricing of primary commodities, under the supervision of the commodity commission of the organization.[22] After the ITO has been established it may be possible to bring the production and marketing of petroleum entering into international trade under some form of international supervision with a view to protecting the interests of consumers and producers alike. However, in the light of current

21. For example, Standard of New Jersey, Socony, and Shell have large markets in the Eastern Hemisphere relative to their share of Middle East oil output, while Anglo-Iranian, Standard of California, Texas, and Gulf control a large potential output but their markets in Europe are relatively small. This situation was the basis for the recent acquisition by Jersey and Socony of a share in the Arabian-American and of the proposed agreement between Jersey and Socony and Anglo-Iranian for sharing the output of Iran.

22. See *Havana Charter*, Chapter VI.

international political conditions, and considering the strong opposition of the American oil industry to any form of control, the prospects of effective international supervision are rather dim. Probably the best that can be hoped for is an international agreement similar to the draft of the Anglo-American Oil Agreement, which would state general principles of fair dealing and provide for an international advisory body.

International action on matters involving relations between oil producing countries and the concessionaire companies offers some significant possibilities. Special commissions set up under an international oil agreement might draw up model concession contracts which would provide for greater protection to both the companies and the producing countries. Exclusive concession contracts in the Middle East have created industrial empires with extraterritorial rights, and these concessions have in certain cases been protected by the diplomatic and military power of the home countries of the concessionaire companies. Conflicts are inevitable when these countries, most of which have only recently evolved as independent national states, seek to obtain greater control over the operations of the foreign companies within their borders. Some of the countries may want to alter their concession contracts with a view to obtaining larger royalties; some may desire a share in the ownership of the oil properties or a share in the foreign exchange proceeds of the petroleum exports in addition to royalty payments; or some countries may seek outright nationalization of the producing facilities. It has been suggested, therefore, that it would be well to have an international organization to deal with these conflicts when they develop or perhaps to forestall them by an alteration of existing concession arrangements, if possible by mutual consent. In view of the recent discussions of this problem in the United Nations Economic and Social Council it is worth while giving brief consideration to one of the concrete proposals for an international petroleum organization.

PROPOSALS OF THE INTERNATIONAL COOPERATIVE ALLIANCE

In August 1947 a representative of the International Cooperative Alliance [23] appeared before the Economic and Social Council of the United Nations to recommend the creation of a world petroleum authority.[24] The principal objective of the ICA in presenting its proposal was to secure fair treatment for cooperatives by the producers of petroleum throughout the world. The proposal is of considerable interest from the standpoint of the general problem of controlling the production and distribution of world petroleum and the reaction of the representatives of the producing and consuming nations to the ICA proposal. The ICA statement emphasized "the immediate need of placing control and administration of the oil resources of the world under an authority of the United Nations, and, as a first step in that direction, the oil resources of the Middle East, by and with the consent of the states involved, these resources to be administered in such a way that cooperative organizations can be assured of receiving an equitable share." The functions of the proposed international petroleum commission were summarized as follows:

(1) To see that oil concessionaires in the Middle East shall operate in the general public interest;

(2) Plan and enforce oil conservation measures (similar to

---

23. The ICA is an international organization of national consumers' cooperative societies representing thirty-nine countries and is a permanent consultant to the Economic and Social Council.

24. The general outlines of a plan for an international petroleum commission were presented to the Fifth Session of the Economic and Social Council in a document entitled "Proposal for the Creation of a United Nations Petroleum Commission under the Authority of the Economic and Social Council," July 19, 1947. (Mimeographed for use of delegates, July 31, 1947). On August 11, 1947, Dr. Thorsten Odhe of the ICA summarized this document in an address before the Economic and Social Council and recommended that the Economic and Employment Commission study the proposal and bring its recommendations before the next session in 1948.—See Verbatim Record of 111th meeting of Ecosoc., Fifth Session, August 11, 1947.

the conservation measures currently in force in the oil-producing states of the United States);

(3) Provide equal access to oil stocks, to assure that all nations, large or small, can buy oil on an equal footing;

(4) Assure that all types of purchasers—governments, cooperative organizations or private corporations—can buy oil on a basis of equality;

(5) Prohibit price discriminations in favor of particular governments or purchasers and assure that all purchasers can buy in adequate quantities;

(6) Serve as a tribunal to adjudicate any oil disputes that might arise.

Under present world political conditions it is almost inconceivable that the major producing nations would hand over their sovereignty with respect to petroleum production and distribution to an international authority. Enforcement of international agreements with respect to the operations of private companies is a matter for individual national governments. International control of production and distribution would require appropriate legislation by the governments of the nationals holding foreign concessions and the governments of the countries in which the concessions were located. Such legislation would undoubtedly meet with violent opposition in the United States and would be contrary to the terms of the concession contracts in most of the countries where the concessions are held. However, it would be necessary to deal with a relatively few petroleum producing companies and these companies (because of their dependence on the diplomatic support of their governments) tend to acquiesce in the policies of their own governments. This fact indicates considerable possibilities for international cooperation on a voluntary basis. At any rate the complexities of the situation should not prevent a thorough study by either the Economic and Social Council or by the ITO when it is established.[25]

25. In the debate which followed the statement of the ICA representative before the Economic and Social Council, the United States delegate, Mr. Willard Thorp, suggested that the problem might

POLITICAL DEVELOPMENTS IN THE MIDDLE EAST.

This discussion of United States foreign policy with respect to Middle East oil would not be complete without some brief mention of recent political developments in that area. During the war the principal political objectives of the United States and Britain were to secure the friendship and cooperation of the peoples and governments of these countries in the prosecution of the war against the Axis and to maintain the vital supply lines through the Suez Canal and the land route across Iran to Russia. Except in Saudi Arabia and Iran, the British were primarily responsible for the political and economic measures taken with respect to the area. The foreign trade of the Middle East and to some extent the establishment of internal economic controls were under the supervision of the Middle East Supply Center. Although the MESC was nominally a joint Anglo-American organization, it was staffed largely by British subjects and its general policies were largely determined by British administrators. In Iran, following the deposing of the Axis-minded Riza Shah in favor of his son, foreign influence over the country was divided between the American, British, and Russian occupying forces, with internal economic and financial controls being administered by the Millspaugh mission.[26]

In most of the Middle Eastern countries—Egypt, Syria,

---

better be handled by the ITO. Norway, France, and China favored a resolution to the effect that the Economic and Employment Commission study the problem, while the U.K. and the U.S.S.R. recommended that the matter be dropped. The U.K. representative argued that the proposal was highly impractical and proposed that the Council should do no more than take note of the proposal. This resolution was adopted by a vote of 8 to 2, the United States voting with the U.K.—See *Verbatim Record*, 112th Meeting of the Fifth Session of the Economic and Social Council, August 12, 1947.

26. For an account of the activities of the Millspaugh mission see *Americans in Persia*, by H. C. Millspaugh, The Brookings Institution, 1946.

Lebanon, Iraq, and Iran—there were direct interferences with the sovereignty of the national governments on the part of the Allied powers.[27] Only Turkey, Saudi Arabia and the Yemen (which remained completely isolated from the war) maintained their independence. Mention has already been made of the British and American subsidies and loans to Ibn Saud.[28] This aid was provided in part for the purpose of maintaining civil order among the Arab tribes, but it was also inspired in considerable measure by the fact of American petroleum interests in the country.

The three most significant postwar political developments in the Middle East are: (1) the threat of Russian economic and political penetration; (2) the controversy over Palestine; and (3) the upsurge of Arab nationalism. All three of these complex political developments are related to the question of oil and undoubtedly the policies of the United States Government with respect to them are to a degree influenced by the existence of American-owned oil resources in this area. Although a comprehensive discussion of these problems is beyond the scope of this book, a few general observations may be in order. First of all it would be incorrect to attribute the recent diplomatic and economic actions of the United States with respect to the Middle East solely, or even primarily, to our petroleum interests. For example, the Greek-Turkish aid program, which involved among other things a grant of $100 million for the modernization of the Turkish Army, would probably have been put forward by the United

27. In Egypt the British Ambassador forced the King to appoint a pro-Allied Prime Minister, Nahas Pasha; in Iraq the British Army put down an Axis-inspired revolution; and Syria and Lebanon were under French administration until 1945.
28. Saudi Arabia received more direct lend-lease assistance from the United States than any other Middle Eastern country except Turkey. Direct lend-lease to Saudi Arabia totaled $17.5 million dollars and in addition over 22 million ounces of silver were made available on a reimbursable basis. British wartime financial assistance to Saudi Arabia has been estimated at nearly $50 million.

States Administration even if there were no oil in the Middle East. Likewise United States diplomatic support of Iran in refusing to grant an oil concession to the U.S.S.R. was in line with our general policy of preserving the independence of sovereign states. The Middle East is more than an oil reserve; it is a strategic area in the geopolitics of global defense.

In a similar way petroleum cannot be said to dominate other aspects of United States foreign policy with respect to the Middle East. For example, the United States in November 1947 voted in the General Assembly of the United Nations for the partition of Palestine, in spite of vehement objections and threats on the part of the Arab nations. Although the government was insistent upon what it believed to be a proper distribution of the land area between the Arab and Jewish states and upon fair economic treatment of the Palestinian Arabs, the United States delegate voted for what his government believed to be a reasonable solution of the problem. In this connection it is rather unlikely that the Arab states will carry out the threats made by some Arab leaders to cancel foreign oil concessions, since it would be impossible for these countries to operate the concessions themselves. Also the countries are highly dependent upon oil royalties to meet their governmental expenditures and to carry out their development plans.

The third political development mentioned above, the rise of Arab nationalism, coupled with the withdrawal of the British from Egypt and Palestine and the French from the Levant, presents both an opportunity and a responsibility for the United States. Sometimes the withdrawal of foreign powers from politically immature countries creates something of a vacuum which needs to be filled if social stability and economic progress are to be achieved. Many of these countries not only need loans and direct foreign investments to develop their industries and resources, but they need technical advisors and friendly diplomatic council from a world power which they believe they can trust. The United States is ideally suited for this role because of its lack of imperialistic designs on this area, past or present. Moreover, our petroleum interests provide an important common interest which can be made the basis for close political and economic cooperation with the new independent national states of the Middle East.

CHAPTER VIII

PROSPECTS AND CONCLUSIONS

IN THE COURSE of the preceding chapters a number of matters were discussed which have an important bearing on the determination of a foreign oil program for the United States. Although these questions concern our own petroleum policy with respect to all foreign producing areas where American interests are active, they are of particular significance for the Middle East for two important reasons. First, the Middle East is potentially the largest producer of petroleum in the world; and second, it is with respect to the production and marketing of oil from this area that the greatest amount of conflict with other nations, both as consumers and as producers, is likely to arise. It will be our purpose in this chapter to indicate a few tentative conclusions with regard to the following fundamental questions of American foreign petroleum policy: (1) Is direct government participation in foreign oil development necessary to achieve our petroleum objectives? (2) What can be accomplished by means of international petroleum agreements and joint commissions? (3) What should be the basic criteria for the determination of United States petroleum export and import policy? It will be readily admitted that volumes might be written on each one of these questions and that complete answers call for comprehensive studies by specialists in this field. However, the following observations may at least serve to indicate the general character of the studies which ought to be made in this important segment of our foreign economic policy.

In considering these fundamental questions the following facts regarding our domestic petroleum position should be borne in mind. Although there is considerable uncertainty and

PROSPECTS AND CONCLUSIONS

disagreement concerning the availability of petroleum in the United States, the general area of agreement may be summed up as follows:

(1) Proved oil reserves within continental United States are about 22 billion barrels and these reserves are being produced at the rate of over 9 per cent per year.

(2) The discovery rate has fallen off since 1938 despite intensified search, and additional reserves are being found only at steadily increasing cost. It is generally agreed that the United States will be fortunate if it can increase the current level of production of over $5\frac{1}{2}$ million barrels per day (some experts forecast a maximum efficient rate of production for the United States of $3\frac{1}{2}$ million barrels per day by 1965).

(3) By 1965 the demand for petroleum products in the United States is estimated to be over 7 million barrels per day. This means that by 1965 the United States will probably need to import or produce synthetically from one-fourth to one-half of its liquid fuel requirements.

(4) Synthetic production of gasoline from coal and oil shale could supply almost any conceivable demand in the United States for centuries, but at a substantial increase in cost over imported crude. Synthetic production of gasoline from natural gas is already competitive with production from petroleum but the supply of natural gas is limited. (Gasoline from coal or oil shale could probably be produced in competition with gasoline refined from petroleum if the price of domestic crude remains at or above its present level of $2.65 per barrel.)

It will be seen from the above summary that the petroleum position of the United States is by no means desperate. We shall be able to meet any emergency within our own borders provided reasonable conservation measures are taken and provided plans are made, including the construction of emergency facilities for the synthetic production of gasoline. In the meantime United States import policy will need to be geared to our general production, discovery, and conservation policy with respect to domestic oil resources.

THE ISSUE OF DIRECT GOVERNMENT PARTICIPATION

A certain degree of reliance on imports of crude oil is desirable both from the standpoint of conservation and of providing for domestic fuel requirements at reasonable prices to the American consumer. Even if it be admitted that we cannot rely on foreign sources in time of war,[1] conservation of domestic resources may be necessary in order to assure adequate supplies in periods of emergency. The principal question to be decided in judging the merits of government participation in foreign oil operations is whether or not such participation is needed to assure access to the required foreign supplies. In time of war or other national emergencies all of our strategic industries at home or abroad undergo a *de facto* nationalization and their operations are made in one way or another to conform to national policy. Hence, the argument for government ownership of foreign oil facilities must be based on a better realization of our policy objectives in normal times. The possible objectives which the government might want to achieve through government ownership of foreign facilities may be outlined as follows: [2]

(1) The government may want a more rapid development of the foreign concession than is contemplated by private owners either by reason of their financial ability to construct production, refining, and transportation facilities or because world market conditions would not warrant such development in terms of profit and loss calculations.[3]

---

1. Although enemy interference with our lines of communication to foreign fields may prevent oil from reaching continental United States, the oil may still be utilized by our military and naval forces in the area.

2. It is assumed that government ownership as an end in itself is not desired, but that direct government participation in foreign oil operations is considered as a necessary departure from the fundamental policy of private enterprise at home and abroad.

3. The owners may want to hold the oil as an idle reserve until they have utilized their reserves in other fields.

PROSPECTS AND CONCLUSIONS 113

(2) The government may want to prevent a too rapid exhaustion of the reserves of American-owned concessions.

(3) The government may want to secure protection of the concession against encroachment by a third power or violation of the concession agreement by the govenment of the country in which it is located.

(4) The government may want to make certain that it is not overcharged for oil for military uses.

(5) The government may desire to acquire large foreign oil reserves and production facilities to be employed as a yardstick in regulating monopoly prices and in combatting restrictive practices in the international market for petroleum.

(6) The government may want to control the distribution of petroleum from foreign fields as a means of implementing its foreign economic policy. The purpose may be to assure all nations of a fair supply of oil in accordance with an international agreement, or it may want to restrict oil shipments to certain countries as an economic sanction against certain countries, either unilaterally or in concert with other nations.

Except for the first two objectives which concern the rate of utilization of the concessions, all of them could just as well be realized through the establishment of machinery for consultation and cooperation between the government and the industry and through international agreements. Whether or not government ownership is necessary to guarantee the utilization of foreign oil reserves at a rate appropriate to the national interest as determined by the Federal Administration would depend upon the circumstances involved in each case. Financial inability of the concession companies could probably be dealt with by means of government loans, the terms of which could be arranged so that the legitimate interests of other American companies would be protected. It may also be desirable for the government to follow the domestic practice of acquiring an option from foreign concession holders to a portion of their oil reserves for the use of our military forces, including an agreement on the terms of sale of the product. Such arrangements would assure the government adequate supplies of petroleum from foreign sources at reasonable prices.[4] In order to avoid the charge of discrimination the government might offer to negotiate similar agreements with all foreign concession holders. In the event that an American concern was not developing an important foreign concession at a rate deemed appropriate to our national interest, every effort ought to be made to achieve the desired objective by negotiation with the company. If such negotiations fail, consideration might be given to outright purchase, but recent developments indicate that this action is not required in the case of the American-owned concessions in Saudi Arabia and Kuwait. Moreover, the advantages of direct participation would have to be weighed against the disadvantages of a departure from our fundamental policy with respect to state trading and government interference in private industry.

Turning to the argument for government ownership on the grounds that it would enable the United States to provide better diplomatic and military protection to foreign sources of stragetic materials, it appears to the authors that the identical measures are open to us in the case of either private or government ownership.[5] In fact there may be greater flexibility in the use of governmental powers under private ownership. For example, private companies might be able to exert greater pressure in dealing with friendly countries than our government would deem appropriate if it were the owner of the oil concession.

The problem of dealing with restrictive and discriminatory practices in the international market for petroleum is a most difficult and complicated one. No one would deny the existence of a tight oligopoly in the foreign petroleum field and

4. During the course of the hearings before the Senate War Investigating Committee in 1947 charges were made by several witnesses that the United States Navy was overcharged by the Arabian-American Oil Company during the war. (See Chapter IX for a discussion of these charges.)

5. During the 1920's the government used its military power to protect private interests in Latin America.

PROSPECTS AND CONCLUSIONS 115

there is ample evidence that cooperation (or collusion) among the principal firms exists.[6] Even in the absence of specific agreements truly competitive conditions are impossible in a market controlled by only a few firms since each firm must take account of the reactions of his competitors to his own price and production policies. The oil companies learned many years ago that the way to prevent cutthroat competition is to follow common price policies and to respect one another's marketing territories. In addition to the small number of firms, there are certain special characteristics of the international petroleum market which limit competition. Most of the large petroleum-consuming countries have either nationalized their petroleum refining and marketing industries or exercise comprehensive controls over the activities of private companies. Moreover a large portion of the foreign oil produced is marketed by the producing companies themselves.

United States Government ownership of foreign oil-producing resources and facilities might be helpful in eliminating discrimination against certain foreign consumers. By selling to

6. The following is a quotation from a report of the Swedish Government Committee on the present conditions of markets for petroleum products (published in 1946): "In the course of meetings with representatives of the importing firms and by submitting an extensive collection of documents to scrutinization we have been able to state that collaboration between the importing firms has taken place in different respects, i.e., regarding the creation of market quotas, prices, offers to customers, fixing of rebates, relations to cooperative organizations of customers, exclusive agreements with customers, transfers of customers, etc. In this conjunction it should be stated that this collaboration in its main parts is based on international agreements, one of which—with the title of 'Draft Memorandum of Principles'—has been reprinted in our report; this agreement affects Standard, Shell and B. P. Combines."

The above quotation was reproduced in a statement presented by the International Cooperative Alliance before the Economic and Social Council in July, 1947. The "Draft Memorandum of Principles" refers to a secret agreement of 1928 entered into by the Standard Oil Co. (N. J.), Dutch Shell, Anglo-Iranian, and other British interests dealing with the division of world petroleum markets, which the Swedish committee discovered in the course of its investigation.

American marketing companies the government might establish a yardstick for such sales. On the other hand the bulk of the Middle East oil coming into this country will probably be marketed directly by the companies in control of the foreign production. Protection of the American consumer therefore could probably best be achieved by the enforcement of our anti-trust laws covering agreements on oil for sale in the United States.

So far as the protection of foreign consumers against price exploitation and discrimination is concerned, it is doubtful whether this objective is sufficiently important to warrant nationalization of all or a part of our foreign oil production. From a technical standpoint private industry has on the whole done a good job in exploring and developing foreign oil. Government ownership and operation of foreign concessions would be faced with many handicaps which might very well weaken our international petroleum position. The solution to the problems raised by the international cartelization of petroleum lies elsewhere.

THE MECHANISM OF INTERNATIONAL
CONTROL

We have already discussed the limited objectives of the Anglo-American oil agreement, but this agreement is largely concerned with a broad statement of principles and does not deal in an effective way with such questions as: (1) access on equal terms to petroleum and petroleum products by all countries; (2) the handling of disputes over concession contracts and the introduction of terms in future and existing concession contracts which would protect the welfare of both the countries in which oil is produced and the oil companies; (3) the proper utilization of the world's oil resources; and (4) the avoidance of restrictive and discriminatory practices on the part of oil companies. Some discussion was devoted to each of these problems in the preceding chapters. What we are concerned with at this point is the extent to which it is possible under present conditions to deal effectively with these problems by means of international agreements and organizations.

The first question concerns the degree of contol which governments should exercise over their nationals operating in a foreign country, since legal authority rests ultimately with national governments and not with international commissions. There are a number of legal difficulties involved in controlling the activities of American-owned companies operating in foreign fields. Some of the firms are incorporated in other countries, such for example as the Bahrein Petroleum Co., incorporated in Canada, and the California-Texas Oil Co., incorporated in the Bahamas. Doubtless any attempt to control the activities of United States incorporated firms operating abroad would lead them to seek charters elsewhere. Control could of course be exercised by the countries in which the concessions are located, but concession contracts usually stipulate that the concession country shall not interfere with the production and sale of the petroleum. Moreover, it is unlikely that Saudi Arabia or Iran, for example, would be willing to force the producing companies to agree to an alteration of their concession contacts in order to bring the activities of the companies under international supervision. But even if we assume that the legal difficulties involved in company control can be surmounted, the present attitude of Congress toward international control of the petroleum industry either at home or abroad makes an international agreement for this purpose unthinkable in peacetime. The following reservation adopted by the Senate Foreign Relations Committee in approving the Anglo-American Oil Agreement undoubtedly expresses the viewpoint of the vast majority of congressmen: [7] "The Government of the United States does not, either explicitly or inferentially, by the act of ratification of the Anglo-American oil

7. *Senate Foreign Relations Committee Report on the Anglo-American Oil Agreement,* July 7, 1947. This reservation, together with the other two reservations reprinted in the Appendix, were proposed by the American Petroleum Institute and later agreed to by the Department of State.

treaty, subscribe to the principle that any world organization either embracing or not embracing United States membership shall be empowered to review or revise the lawfully acquired concessions, rights, and contracts of American nationals engaged in foreign operations, or to regulate or control the operations of American nationals thereon or thereunder, nor is the act of ratification to be construed as the first step in an international plan or program designed to eventuate in or be supplemented by further and additional international oil treaties having any power to control or regulate the operations of American nationals engaged in the foreign or domestic oil business, or with power to review or revise the lawfully acquired right and concessions and contracts of American nationals or to perform any functions save and except those of a purely advisory nature, without power of enforcement or compulsion."

A final obstacle to compulsory control over trade practices in the international marketing of petroleum lies in the difficulty of proving the existence of collusive action involving restrictive practices among the large producers and of prosecuting the offenders. Members of any illegal international agreement would be subject to two or more jurisdictions and a host of legal complexities would be involved in assembling evidence and bringing the offenders to trial.

Perhaps the most feasible solution to the problem of international control at the present time lies in the establishment of an international advisory commission, leaving to each government the acceptance or rejection of the recommendations and the means of carrying out such recommendations as are accepted. This is admittedly a far cry from an international petroleum authority, but such an arrangement would be better than nothing. Recommendations of the commission which had a chance of success would probably be favored by the countries whose nationals control the bulk of the world's production. In the case of certain of those countries the governments themselves already either own or maintain a close control over their foreign oil-producing interests. (For example, the British Government has a controlling interest in Anglo-Iranian and the French Government holds 35 per cent of the Cie. Francaise des Petroles which owns a quarter interest in the Iraq Petroleum Company.) In the case of the United States, American companies operating abroad can in general be counted on to abide by the wishes of the government with respect to their dealings with other governments or their nationals. This has been the case in the past (and is likely to be even more so in the future) because of their dependence upon the diplomatic support of the government in foreign negotiations. In most cases therefore the recommendations of an international advisory body could be implemented by voluntary cooperation between the American industry and the government.

THE VALUE OF INTERNATIONAL PETROLEUM AGREEMENTS

Having reached certain conclusions on the feasibility of various methods of international control, we will now turn briefly to the question of what might be accomplished through an international petroleum agreement. Until such time as nations are willing to relinquish a greater amount of their sovereignty than they are at present, the principal value of international economic conferences and commissions will lie in the opportunity which they provide for orderly discussion and negotiation on common problems. International agreements on broad principles are of little value unless they provide for the setting up of continuing commissions whose function is to reach agreements and make recommendations on emerging problems and conflicts. The statements of principles involved in most international conventions are so broad and so carefully hedged that they are of little real value for the solution of concrete issues.

An international petroleum commission should be composed of representatives of governments which are parties to an international petroleum convention providing for rather broad terms of reference for the work of the commission. The commission's functions should include that of investigation, the publication of reports and the making of specific recommendations to governments. The commission should be free to investigate complaints and consider proposals transmitted to it by governments or by non-governmental consultative bodies. The latter would consist of representatives of various branches of the petroleum industry—producers and marketers —and of consumer groups such as the International Cooperative Alliance. Each member nation might also have representative advisory groups which would be consulted by the government in considering recommendations of the international commissions. The matter of enforcement of recommendations with respect to the companies themselves would be left to each nation having jurisdiction over them.

The existence of such an international commission would provide a sounding board for airing complaints on the part of oil consuming countries dissatisfied with the policies of the international oil companies owning the concessions. It would help to bring out into the open production and marketing agreements of the producing companies and subject them to the criticism of the commission. It would provide a mechanism by which international agreements covering conservation, production, marketing, and prices could be reached under the auspices of the commission. In the absence of an inter-governmental mechanism secret agreements or tacit understandings are likely to be reached by the handful of large companies controlling the bulk of the world's production and marketing of petroleum outside of the United States. It is better that such arrangements be made under the auspices of an international body in which the public interest is represented. Finally an international petroleum commission could perform a valuable service in making recommendations with respect to the terms of concession contracts and by offering its services as an arbiter of disputes arising under such contracts.

There are in general three means by which an international commission of the type described above might be established. First, the United States and Britain might invite other nations to become partners to the Anglo-American Oil Agreement, or perhaps one similar to it which would be drafted in advance by the two governments. This would be the quickest way to get a document, but probably would not be satisfactory to other countries, which would want to have a hand in its drafting. Another way would be to set up a petroleum commodity council in accordance with the provisions of the proposed ITO Charter,[8] which would operate under the supervision of the ITO. A third method would be for the Economic and Social Council to call a United Nations conference for the drafting of a charter for an international petroleum organization which would become another semi-independent constituent organization of the United Nations.

Although there may be a number of political and administrative factors with which the authors are not familiar, it appears to us at the present time that the third method is the most satisfactory. Unless the United Nations becomes completely ineffective and inoperative, the initiative for the establishment of an international petroleum organization should be taken by that body rather than by one or two countries alone. Although the organization could be established within the ITO, there are several reasons why we believe a separate organization is preferable. First of all the problem is sufficiently important and specialized in character to warrant the setting up of a separate organization. The commodity agreements and commodity councils provided for under the ITO Charter are designed to deal with burdensome surpluses of primary commodities by means of temporary agreements covering production, prices, and marketing conditions. The functions of an international petroleum commission, as proposed above, are much broader than the ITO commodity councils. The ITO Charter does lay down certain principles regarding the use of restrictive business practices and members of the ITO undertake certain obligations with respect to the enforcement of regulations concerning restrictive business practices. How-

8. See above, Chapter VI.

ever, in the light of the present structure of the international market for petroleum these regulations are in some respects unrealistic and incapable of enforcement. At any rate a special set of principles ought to be developed with reference to the particular problems of the petroleum industry. Finally, there may very well be countries which would be willing to join an international petroleum organization which for one reason or another may not become members of the ITO.

UNITED STATES EXPORT AND IMPORT POLICIES

United States petroleum import and export policies will have an important bearing on the development of foreign production, including that of the Middle East. For example a long-run policy of conserving United States oil reserves in favor of large imports from abroad would tend to hasten the expansion of foreign output. On the other hand a policy of self-sufficiency including perhaps a substantial reliance on synthetic production to meet the deficiency in our domestic requirements would lessen the rate of foreign expansion. Barring a severe depression in the United States in the next few years, however, the short-run outlook for foreign production is one of rapid expansion limited only by the availability of refining and transportation facilities.

During 1947 United States exports and imports of petroleum and petroleum products were approximately balanced. The high level of domestic and foreign demand necessitated the reimposition of export controls on most petroleum products, and controls will probably have to be maintained until the world supply situation eases.[9] In 1946 exports of petroleum and petroleum products from the United States were 3 per cent of domestic production as compared with 6 per cent for 1938. The Report of the Committee for European Economic Cooperation (CEEC) calls for imports from the Western Hemisphere and other sources which may be somewhat

9. First Quarterly Report under the Second Decontrol Act of 1947, Department of Commerce, 1947.

larger than can be supplied without reducing United States domestic consumption. In addition the CEEC Report envisages a 150 per cent increase in the refining capacity of the participating countries, an estimate which is also believed to be overoptimistic in light of the availability of materials over the next four years. However, if the Middle East pipe lines to the Mediterranean can be completed on schedule by 1953 and if there is a general easing of equipment and transport shortages, the CEEC petroleum goals may be realized within reasonable limits early in the 1950's. The CEEC countries expect to increase their consumption of petroleum products to about 1,500,000 b/d by 1951 as compared with 750,000 b/d in 1938. The European Recovery Program calls for a gradual increase in petroleum to be supplied by the Middle East at the expense of imports from the Western Hemisphere. Thus American aid under the European Recovery Program will hasten the development of Middle East oil by providing refinery equipment for processing the oil, tankers for its transportation, and oil burning equipment for its utilization in Europe.

Once the present world shortage of petroleum comes to an end with the expansion of Middle East production, the need for United States export controls will probably disappear, regardless of America's oil objectives. Both transportation costs to Europe and production costs in Middle East fields will be lower than in the United States so that in a few years United States oil, with the exception of a few specialized products, will no longer be competitive in world markets with oil from other sources. There remains, however, the question of United States import policy as an important factor in foreign development over the long run. Even if the United States should not import substantial quantities of petroleum from the Middle East, our import policy will in large measure determine the size of the Western Hemisphere surplus (if any) which will compete with Middle East oil in the Eastern Hemisphere.

Protection of the American petroleum industry dates from

1932, when a great increase in discoveries coincided with depressed domestic conditions. The Revenue Act of 1932 provided for an excise tax of 21 cents a barrel on crude and $1.05 on gasoline. Our imports in the next seven years were cut in half. In 1939 a trade agreement with Venezuela reduced these duties by 50 per cent but imposed a quota of 5 per cent of domestic production on crude imports.[10] The Mexican trade agreement of 1943 removed the quota and imports have climbed steadily since then under the impetus of the war shortage.[11] Without the removal of restrictions the war effort might have been seriously hampered in 1945 because the United States was producing at the greatest capacity possible without seriously damaging its fields.

Although the determination of an appropriate petroleum import policy for the United States is outside the scope of this book, a few general observations will be made with regard to the development of an appropriate program. First of all, our petroleum import program should be integrated with our domestic production, discovery, and conservation programs, including experimentation with synthetic fuels and the establishment of pilot plants. The development of such a program should be assigned to experts in various branches of the industry and not to congressional committees trying to find their way through a maze of conflicting testimony. The principal consideration in determining a proper import policy for the United States is the conservation of our oil reserves so that they will be available in the event that foreign sources are denied to us. The American public should not be taxed in the form of oil tariffs simply to protect the revenues of domestic petroleum producers. Conservation re-

10. The quota was first set voluntarily by the principal importers to avoid depressing the domestic market and was incorporated into the NIRA Code.

11. The Independent Petroleum Association of America has recently filed a brief with the State Department demanding restoration of 1932 import duties and a quota system limiting imports to that amount which cannot be produced at the MER of domestic fields. *National Petroleum News*, Dec. 25, 1946, p. 17.

quires that domestic production should be limited. However, it is feared that unlimited imports might make large numbers of marginal wells uneconomical to operate and their abandonment would perhaps render the oil permanently unrecoverable. It is also argued that unless we maintain the domestic price of crude, wildcatting will be restricted and new reserves will not be discovered and developed. Our import policy must therefore provide a proper balance between the conservation of existing reserves and the stimulation of a rate of discovery and production appropriate to meet an emergency in which we might find it necessary to supply our entire needs from domestic sources.

In our opinion, however, these objectives should not be attained by means of a tariff or an import quota. Both of these methods result in higher prices to domestic consumers and windfall profits to the producers. They are essentially shotgun expedients and are not designed to attain the particular objectives at the least possible cost to the American public. They are also at variance with the international trade policies which the United States is trying to promote through the International Trade Organization and its Reciprocal Trade Agreements. A more efficient and desirable method is to be found in the use of subsidies to private industry to stimulate the discovery of new petroleum reserves. During the war the government subsidized production from marginal oil wells as a means of preventing a rise in OPA ceiling prices of petroleum products. The Reconstruction Finance Corporation also used subsidies to stimulate production of copper, lead, and other metals during the war with considerable saving to the government over what it would have cost to permit a general rise in the ceiling price.[12] Wildcatting and production from marginal wells could be stimulated by a judicious use of subsidies while at the same time maintaining domestic prices near world levels. In answer to the charge that this is government interference in the oil industry, the use of subsidies is no more

12. See "Subsidies and Price Control," by R. F. Mikesell and C. E. Galbreath, *American Economic Review*, September, 1942, 524-37.

of an interference than the indirect subsidy to the entire industry which is involved in the imposition of a tariff.

Higher domestic prices secured by tariffs or quotas are also undesirable in that they encourage a high rate of domestic production of existing reserves. Along with a system of subsidies to encourage wildcatting we suggest that the government acquire newly discovered petroleum reserves and withhold them from production for purposes of conservation. We also suggest that consideration be given to the establishment of a federal agency to supplement the work of the present state proration commissions in order that the United States can evolve a truly national petroleum production program.

Finally, as regards American-owned petroleum fields abroad, it is recommended that every encouragement be given to our foreign producers to expand output both for domestic and foreign requirements. The development of a long-range domestic program would greatly aid foreign producers in planning for the future. The planning of foreign production and oil conservation might also be implemented by the federal government acquisition of options on foreign oil reserves from private concession holders, together with an understanding regarding the price to be paid by the government for oil from these reserves. Planning with respect to production for the world market could also be facilitated by United States participation in an international petroleum agreement along the lines suggested earlier in this chapter.

CONCLUSION

Our analysis of American policy in relation to Middle East oil has necessarily led us far afield. The conclusions with respect to how much the United States should invest in Middle East oil and how much it should import will depend in part upon our domestic oil program. But the natural market for the vast bulk of Arabian oil is Europe, particularly the countries of western Europe which have practically no petroleum resources of their own. The Western Hemisphere will probably

PROSPECTS AND CONCLUSIONS 127

be self-sufficient in petroleum for some years to come. This fact should not lessen our national interest in the expansion of American production of oil in the Middle East however. Abundant supplies of cheap petroleum from Eastern Hemisphere sources will contribute to the recovery and eventual prosperity of Europe. America's economic and political interest in the welfare of Europe is evidenced by the sacrifice which this country is willing to make in providing billions of dollars in aid under the European Recovery Program.

The United States also has a more general international interest in an abundant supply of petroleum for the peoples of the world as a whole. This interest requires the proper utilization and conservation of the oil resources in American hands all over the world and the distribution of oil on a fair and equitable basis. It may also imply a willingness to permit access by other countries to a share in the undiscovered oil resources of the world.

In the light of the above general policy conclusions the following proposals with respect to United States oil policy in the Middle East are suggested:

(1) Because of the pressing world demand the United States should encourage the rapid development of the productive capacity of the Persian Gulf oil fields and the facilities for transporting this oil to market. Such encouragement would include continued diplomatic assistance to the American oil companies and the establishment of high priorities for materials for productive equipment and pipe lines.

(2) There should be established as soon as possible a free market for petroleum in the Persian Gulf. So long as supplies are limited in relation to demand a fair method of distribution should be worked out, preferably by international agreement. If a free market were created by the private companies, the most important argument for international control would be disposed of.

(3) The Anglo-American oil pact should be ratified in order to provide a formal basis for cooperation. This pact

might then be broadened to include other countries in an agreement along much the same lines.

(4) A more comprehensive international agreement covering rates of production, marketing practices, access to undeveloped resources, and relations between the companies and the producing countries may eventually become desirable. When petroleum again becomes abundant, the conservation of the world's oil supplies and the avoidance of over-capacity will assume greater importance. At the present time, however, political obstacles, including the relations between the great powers in the United Nations and the bitter conflict in the Middle East over the future of Palestine, appear to preclude any chance of international control over petroleum. There is also the opposition of the American Congress and of the private oil companies to any extension of governmental controls in this field and a general suspicion of all efforts in the direction of international cooperation. However, all of these obstacles may disappear in time and it may be possible to develop machinery for world cooperation in dealing with a wide range of petroleum problems. As was suggested earlier in this chapter, however, we favor international agreements which provide for the carrying out of recommendations on a voluntary basis rather than the establishment of a world petroleum authority.

CHAPTER IX

SOME RECENT DEVELOPMENTS

SINCE FEBRUARY 1948 when the foregoing chapters were completed, political and economic events affecting the future of Arabian oil have moved rapidly. The serious political disturbances in the Middle East have interfered with both current operations and planning for the future. The important refinery at Haifa has been shut down since April, 1948. Since the refinery is controlled by Israel and the Haifa branch of the pipe line carrying the crude from the Iraqi wells lies in Arab territory, production cannot be resumed even for export until a settlement between the two conflicting parties can be reached.[1]

Perhaps even more serious for the long run is the delay in the construction of the pipe lines from the Persian Gulf fields. In December 1947 all work was halted on the Trans-Arabian pipe line in Syria, Lebanon, and Trans-Jordan, although work on the Persian Gulf end continued. The Syrian Parliament had earlier refused to ratify an agreement for laying the pipe line across her territory to Sidon, which was to be the terminus of the line from Ras Tanura in Arabia. It was reported that the Arab League had passed a resolution to the effect that no American company would be permitted to lay pipe across the borders of member states until the United States Government altered its policy with respect to Palestine. It has also been reported in the press that Egypt would like to see the terminus of the line at the Gulf of Aqaba on the Red Sea, and

---

1. Some of the information and data included in this chapter became available just before this book was printed and hence are in certain cases at variance with earlier estimates and factual information found in the preceding chapters.

the establishment of a large refinery in Egypt operated jointly by Aramco and the Egyptian Government. One disadvantage of this arrangement is that, although it would save many hundreds of miles of tanker transport, shipments to Europe would have to pay the toll for passage through the Suez Canal. Moreover, no decision can be made with respect to the terminus since Egypt is also bound by the decision of the Arab League. Our latest information from Aramco officials is that the company still plans to terminate the pipe line in Sidon (Lebanon) and expects the Syrian Parliament to ratify the agreement for transit rights. Plans also call for a large refinery at the Sidon terminus.

Pending clarification of the political situation in the Middle East the United States has suspended all licensing of steel pipe and other construction materials for the Trans-Arabian pipe line. About 53,000 tons of steel pipe had been licensed for this project up to mid-1948. However, export licenses are being granted for other Middle East petroleum projects. The Bahrein refinery is being expanded with U. S. materials, from a present capacity of 117,000 b/d to a capacity of 142,000 b/d. Steel pipe is also being exported for the construction of a 20-22 inch line in Iran from the Agha Jari field to a deep-water port at Bandar Mashur.[2]

Despite the political differences of the Arab States with the United States, relations between the Arabian Government and Aramco appear to be harmonious. It has been reported in the press that after lengthy negotiations the long-standing dispute over the payment of royalties has been settled. It will be recalled that the concession contract calls for payment in gold pounds (British sovereigns) or the equivalent in sterling or dollar exchange. During the war sovereigns became scarce and royalty payments were made largely in dollars.[3] The dispute between Aramco and the Arabian Government con-

2. *Export Control and Allocation Powers* (Fourth Quarterly Report of the Secretary of Commerce), August, 1948, pp. 45-46.

3. The price of gold sovereigns in terms of Saudi Arabian riyals and other Middle East currencies rose to more than double the New York and London official rate of $8.24. The Saudi Arabian Govern-

cerned whether the gold sterling pound should be valued at the London and New York official rate of $8.24 or at the market rate in Saudi Arabia, (which has fluctuated between $10 to $20 per pound) in determining the equivalent in dollar exchange. The price finally agreed upon was reported to be $12 per gold pound.[4] The royalty fixed in the concession agreement was 4 shillings gold per ton of crude, which at $12 per pound sterling gives us a rate of $2.40 or 32 cents per barrel. (When paid in dollars the rate is 10 cents less per ton or 30.8 cents per barrel.) At the present time, however, Aramco is paying royalties in sovereigns which it acquires at a price approximating the official rate of $8.24. Hence, so long as the company is able to acquire gold sovereigns at the official rate the effective royalty rate will be no more than 22 cents per barrel.

Political developments have apparently not hampered the efforts of American companies to obtain additional concessions in the Middle East. In July 1948 it was announced that the Sheikh of Kuwait had granted a concession to the American Independent Oil Company for exploration and development in Kuwait's undivided half interest in the neutral zone between Kuwait and Saudi Arabia.[5] Since Aramco holds rights from Saudi Arabia over the latter's half interest in the neutral zone there will have to be an understanding between these two companies before operations can begin. It is reported that the American Independent, representing several U. S. companies, none of which have other interests in the Middle East, will insist on independence with respect to pro-

---

ment argued that since many of its expenses were payable in gold sovereigns it should be paid the royalty of 4 shillings gold per ton of oil at a rate in dollars equivalent to the higher market value of sovereigns in Saudi Arabia.

4. *Le Commerce du Levant,* Beirut, Lebanon, June 26, 1948.

5. *New York Times,* July 7, 1948, p. 1. The American Independent is reported to have outbid nine major companies in securing the concession and to have agreed to a royalty of $.35 per barrel—the highest in the Middle East. Other terms of the agreement were reported to be a $7 million bonus, an annual rental of $600,000 until oil is discovered, and a block of stock in the company.

duction and distribution policies in the operations in the Kuwait neutral zone.[6] This is highly desirable from the standpoint of the foreign oil policy of the United States government, which favors a reduction in the degree of concentration of control.

SENATE HEARINGS ON NAVY OIL PURCHASES

After lengthy hearings, in April 1948 the U. S. Senate Special Committee Investigating the National Defense Program, under the chairmanship of Senator Brewster, made public a report on Navy purchases of Middle East oil.[7] In its *Report* the committee has concluded that the U. S. Navy was grossly overcharged by Aramco for purchases of oil during the war, particularly in light of the large amount of U. S. Government financial assistance to the Saudi-Arabian Government which the committee alleges was for the purpose of protecting Aramco's concession. The conclusions of the committee are quoted as follows: [8]

1. The United States Government extended direct and indirect lend-lease and other assistance to the Saudi Arabian Government in excess of $99,000,000 of which only approximately $27,000,000 is likely to be recovered.

2. These advances of direct and indirect lend-lease and other assistance to the Saudi Arabian Government were initiated for the most part by the Arabian American Oil Co., its affiliates, and parent companies, for two reasons: First, in 1941, to relieve themselves of the onerous burden of supplying large funds to

---

6. *New York Times*, July 7, 1948. The American Independent Oil Company was incorporated in Delaware in August 1947, with an authorized capitalization of $100,000,000. The incorporators are J. S. Abercrombie, Houston, Tex.; Allied Oil Company, Inc., Cleveland; Ashland Oil and Refining Company, Ashland, Ky.; Deep Rock Oil Corporation of Chicago; Globe Oil and Refining Company of Wichita, Kan.; Hancock Oil Company, Long Beach, Calif.; Phillips Petroleum Company, Bartlesville, Okla.; Signal Oil and Gas Company, Los Angeles, Calif.; and Sunray Oil Company, Tulsa, Okla.

7. *Additional Report of the Special Committee Investigating the National Defense Program*, April 28, 1948.

8. *Ibid.*, p. 32.

SOME RECENT DEVELOPMENTS 133

meet the budgetary requirements of Saudi Arabia; and second, in 1943 direct United States lend-lease was requested by the company to eliminate the danger of its concessions and earnings falling under the financial control of the United Kingdom.

3. To induce the grant of aid to the Saudi Arabian Government, the Arabian American Oil Co. offered to sell to the United States under a proposal to the President dated April 16, 1941 at prices based on fuel oil at 40 cents per barrel. Under another proposal made February 8, 1943, as a further inducement to the United States to extend direct lend-lease to Saudi Arabia, the company offered to set aside reserves and to sell its petroleum products "at prices well under world prices" or at "cost plus a nominal profit."

4. When the United States Government needed oil because of its war demands, notwithstanding these prior proposals, the companies offered the Navy fuel oil at $1.05 a barrel on a take-it-or-leave-it basis. The Navy was forced to buy the oil on these terms. The committee is of the opinion that the oil companies were under a moral if not a legal obligation to disclose to the naval procurement officers their previous proposals for the sale of oil submitted to the President. The oil companies exploited the government by exacting high prices for their products despite the high expenditures and assistance granted to Saudi Arabia at the companies' behest to protect and preserve the companies' concessions.

5. The committee is of the opinion that in paying $1.05 a barrel, the United States Government was overcharged between 30 and 38 million dollars on sales made to the Navy by Aramco and its affiliates, between January 1, 1942, and June 30, 1947, by payment of prices higher than those the oil companies had a right to insist on in the light of their previous dealings with the United States.

6. The committee believes that the Navy Department wholly failed to exercise its wartime procurement authority in not obtaining production cost figures for the Arabian oil fields and in awarding contracts to Aramco and its affiliates at prices which the Navy representatives admitted were excessive.

7. The committee is of the opinion that if the statement contained in the official Navy justification for the purchase of oil at $1.05 a barrel is true, that the oil companies represented to the Navy that they had doubled their royalty payment from 21 to 42 cents a barrel, then the government clearly was defrauded because the royalty payments were not doubled.

8. However, if the statement is false, and the oil companies did not represent to the Navy that their royalty payments were double, then it is obvious that the government overpaid at least 21 cents a barrel, aggregating losses of millions of dollars.

9. Naval procurement of oil from Aramco will continue for an indefinite period. It is impossible to ascertain the final over-all costs of these overcharges and the total loss to the government by its failure to have implemented the Moffett and Rodgers proposals. From the standpoint of national defense the Arabian reserves are of very dubious value. Most military opinion agrees on the probability of the destruction or capture of the Arabian oil fields by the enemy in the event of any crisis.

10. The committee is of the opinion that when companies sell to the United States Government, especially during war, the doctrine of "caveat emptor" should not apply. Companies must be required to deal openly and fairly with the government. In cases where companies fail to do this and a loss results to the government a remedy should be provided to permit recovery.

11. The committee recommends that greater care be exercised by the various governmental departments and agencies where industrial experts are employed to make certain such experts are disqualified from handling matters or determining policy which affects the interest of the companies with which they are or were affiliated.

12. The committee recommends that all government agencies concerned with the procurement of petroleum products should be more closely coordinated. A proper federal agency should be established to administer all government problems concerned with petroleum, both civilian and military. Any agency, however, to be successful must because of the complex and varied nature of the oil industry, both domestic and foreign, have a strong and competent industry advisory group working in closest cooperation. Only by such a combination can proper results be accomplished.

13. The committee recommends that the subject of tax avoidance by the formation of foreign subsidiary companies of United States corporations should receive consideration by the Joint Committee on Internal Revenue Taxation for such study and possible legislative correction as may seem proper.

14. The committee recommends that a continuing investigation of national petroleum affairs be authorized for either a joint committee of the Senate and the House of Representatives or for one committee of the Senate and one committee of the House.

SOME RECENT DEVELOPMENTS 135

15. It is the opinion of the committee that the matter of the purchase of a 40 per cent interest in Aramco by the Standard Oil Co. of New Jersey and Socony-Vacuum Oil Co. with its possible effect of lessening competition in the United States markets should receive the utmost consideration of the Attorney General and any petroleum board or congressional committee that may have jurisdiction.

Any attempt to evaluate the committee's charges with respect to the prices charged the Navy for oil would require information on production costs not available to the authors. As regards the question of the amount of royalties which were being paid it should be pointed out that this question was under dispute throughout the war period and that the Saudi Arabian Government claimed a rate which was more than twice the 21 cents per barrel rate actually being paid by the company. (Legally no royalties were paid since 1941 since the Saudi Arabian Government refused to accept royalties at the 21-cent rate. The company did make advances on account to the government at the 21-cent rate. Until this dispute was settled, therefore, Aramco did not know what its royalty costs would be since presumably any settlement would be retroactive.) It should also be pointed out that until recently the company had paid no dividends and the owners were obliged to provide it with new capital until the end of 1945. Even with a substantial amount of U. S. Government protection it must be admitted that investments in the Middle East are extremely risky in the light of the unstable political conditions in the area. The proper rate of return for an investment of this character is extremely difficult to judge and a complete discussion of this question is beyond the scope of this book.

The committee has probably overstated its case when it alleges that U. S. assistance totalling $99 million was made available to the Saudi Arabian Government primarily to protect the profits of the oil companies. The committee report's breakdown of United States and British financial assistance to Saudi Arabia is as follows: [9]

9. *Report*, op. cit., p. 16.

PROBABLY NONRECOVERABLE

British grants sterling equivalent of approximate		$51,000,000
United States credit lend-lease:		
Joint United States-United Kingdom aid: United States share	$11,000,000	
1945 supplemental United States aid	3,000,000	
1945 United States-United Kingdom military aid; United States share	3,000,000	
Transportation costs on silver approximate	136,000	
Silver lost at sea	733,000	
Total United States lend-lease aid, approximate		17,869,000
Airports constructed at Dhahran and Lauqa after VJ-day, approximate		3,600,000
Total probably nonrecoverable, approximate		72,469,000

PROBABLY RECOVERABLE

United States lend-lease silver bullion	$15,000,000	
United States Export-Import Bank credit	10,000,000	
United States surplus property credit	2,000,000	
Total probably recoverable		27,000,000
Total probably nonrecoverable and probably recoverable		99,469,000

The committee contends that the British financial assistance was actually a form of indirect aid by the United States since our lend-lease assistance to the United Kingdom had to be increased by this amount. Although it is possible to argue that Britain's contribution to Saudi Arabia had some effect upon the former's lend-lease requirements from the United States, the bulk of the assistance took the form of foodstuffs and other commodities acquired in sterling area countries. Be that as it may, the chief purpose of U. S. and British aid, as was pointed out in Chapter VI, was largely for maintaining civil order in this strategic area and for insuring friendly cooperation on the part of the natives. A serious revolt in the Middle Eastern countries might have cost the Allies much more than the lend-lease and other assistance provided and would have required a diversion of military forces at a time when the Germans were at the gates of Cairo. Moreover, we might have lost a strategic source of oil for naval operations in the Far East. In the case of the airfields at Dhahran and Lauqa, these projects were undertaken for purely military reasons. If their completion after V-J day was related to the protection of our oil interests—and there may have been other strategic reasons for constructing them—it must be said that the United States has an interest in Arabian oil which goes far beyond protecting the profits of the Americans who happen to own the investments.

As for the lend-lease silver and the Export-Import Bank and surplus property credits, we have extended similar financial assistance to other governments in which no petroleum interests are involved for reasons of U. S. foreign policy.[10] Moreover, in the case of Saudi Arabia these loans would appear to be amply secured by future royalty payments to the Saudi Arabian Government.

As regards the recommendations of the committee with respect to government procurement of foreign produced oil we have a great deal of sympathy. Better coordination of procurement activities and the formulation of a long-range government foreign petroleum policy is urgently needed. This question has been dealt with in the preceding chapter.

FUTURE CAPACITY AND PROJECTED CAPITAL EXPENDITURES

Given the enormous oil reserves of the Middle East, increased production will depend upon the availability of producing and refining facilities and upon transportation. Current plans announced by the oil companies call for an increase in refining capacity to over a million barrels per day and an expansion of pipe-line facilities to about 2 million barrels per day. The capital expenditures required for these projected facilities total nearly $2 billion, not including a probable ex-

10. Silver was also lend-leased to India for currency purposes during the war.

pansion of facilities in Iran by the Anglo-Iranian Oil Company. Table 4 gives a tentative breakdown of these capital expenditures as estimated by the research staff of the Arabian-American Oil Company. Whether or not these large investment programs can be carried out according to schedule depends in considerable measure upon political developments in the area and also upon the availability of construction materials, the vast bulk of which must come from the United States and the industrial countries of Europe. The kinds of steel needed are among those currently in shortest supply in the United States.

TABLE 4

ESTIMATED CAPITAL EXPENDITURES ON REFINERIES, PIPE LINES, PRODUCING FACILITIES, FOR THE FIVE-YEAR PERIOD 1948-1953 *

Trans-Arabian Pipe Line	$ 200,000,000
Mediterranean Refining Co.	69,000,000
Iraq Petroleum Co. (1-16", 1-30")	180,000,000
Refinery additions, Haifa	25,000,000
Aramco producing facilities	320,000,000
Middle East Pipe Line	230,000,000
Kuwait Eastern Pipe Line	200,000,000
Producing Facilities in:	
Iraq	
Kuwait	
Neutral Zone	
Bahrein	
Qatar	
Trucial Oman	700,000,000
Total	$1,924,000,000

* Aramco staff memo entitled "Oil and the Economic Prosperity of the Middle East," p. 5.

Although the bulk of the investment expenditures will be made for the procurement of foreign materials and the payment for the services of foreign technicians, large amounts of foreign exchange will be spent in the Middle East countries themselves. It has been estimated that over the period 1948-1953 foreign exchange expenditures by oil companies in Middle East countries (excluding Iran and Egypt) will total

SOME RECENT DEVELOPMENTS 139

$155 million annually.[11] An estimated additional $50 million annually will result from local expenditures by foreign staffs and from other sources, so that total annual foreign exchange benefits to these countries may amount to some $200 millions or $12.10 per inhabitant in the countries included in the estimate.

THE PRICING OF ARABIAN OIL

It has been noted that production costs of Arabian oil are substantially below those in the United States. If purely competitive conditions existed in the world market for oil, prices for the same quality of crude would be the same regardless of the source, except for transportation changes. But competitive conditions do not exist and in addition the output of Persian Gulf oil is limited by a lack of processing and transporting facilities. A controversy has arisen over whether the companies operating in the Middle East should price their oil on the basis of U. S. Gulf prices (ranging from $2.65 to $3.00 per barrel) or whether they should charge prices which bear a closer relationship to production cost. This question is of importance to the American public not only as regards Middle East oil which may be imported into this country, but also because it affects the price of oil imported into Europe and financed by ECA dollars.

11. "Oil and the Economic Prosperity of the Middle East," p. 26. These estimated expenditures include direct payments to governments in the form of royalties, taxes, customs duties, etc., as well as payments for local labor, purchases of food and materials, etc. About two-thirds of the foreign exchange payments will be in dollars and the remainder in sterling. These annual expenditures broken down by countries are estimated as follows:

	(in millions of dollars)		(in millions of dollars)
Arabia	76.2	Kuwait	24.4
Iraq	31.9	Bahrein	6.6
Trans-Jordan	1.0	Qatar	.5
Palestine	2.6	Trucial Oman	.5
Syria	4.1	Unassigned until Kuwait	
Lebanon	5.3	P.L. route fixed	1.5
	Total 155.0		

Eugene Holman, President of the Standard Oil Company (N.J.) recently made the following statement in answer to a charge of Senator O'Mahoney that Arabian oil is sold on a world-wide basing point system: [12] "Our announced f.o.b prices for crude oil supplies at the Eastern Mediterranean or Persian Gulf are equivalent to the Caribbean price for crude plus freight at published U. S. Maritime Commission rates from the Caribbean to Western Europe less freight on the same basis from either the Eastern Mediterranean or the Persian Gulf depending on the supply point to Western Europe." (Caribbean prices equal U. S. Gulf prices.)

It is a matter of definition whether this constitutes a basing point system although it contains the essential element common to all basing point systems, namely, the determination of prices in all areas with relation to one base price. The only difference between this system and the basing point pricing of steel, for example, is that f.o.b. sales are also made at points of origin in the Persian Gulf. The price there is calculated so as to equalize the delivered price of oil from any source to Western Europe.

Whatever name may be given to this system of pricing, it is doubtful that a more competitive market situation in the Persian Gulf would produce a lower price until facilities are adequate for suppliers there to take over a larger share of world markets. Under competitive conditions, whatever the costs of Middle Eastern petroleum products, their prices in Europe could not be lower than those of similar Caribbean and American products until tanker, pipe-line, and refinery capacity permit Persian Gulf oil to supplant higher cost sources. Until that time, the only alternative to the present pricing system would be a rationing or allocation scheme which would permit different prices for the same product in the same market. Since producing companies of several nationalities are involved, such a scheme might require special international agreements.

12. Quoted in the *Oil and Gas Journal,* July 15, 1948, p. 56.

SOME RECENT DEVELOPMENTS 141

ARABIAN DEVELOPMENT AND AMERICAN DOMESTIC
OIL SUPPLIES

It has been pointed out that steel and other material sent to the Middle East will permit the production of much more oil than a similar investment in the United States. Some recent calculations fully support this contention. In the United States a ton of steel is required to produce an additional 250 barrels of oil per year, whereas the same amount of steel employed in Saudi Arabia will permit the production of ten times as much oil.[13] It would appear, therefore, that exports of equipment to the Middle East will pay good dividends in terms of relieving the current oil shortage.

Most of the current controversy over steel exports has concerned the building of the Trans-Arabian Pipeline and the other proposed lines. Although political considerations have clouded the issue, the economic argument seems clear enough. The proposed 300,000 b/d pipe line and the 62 tankers which the line would replace would require about the same amount of steel. Since the pipe line has already been started, however, the steel which could now be diverted from use in the pipe line would be sufficient for only two-thirds of this tanker capacity. When the line is increased to its full capacity of 500,000 b/d by the addition of more pumping stations, the saving in steel in comparison to the equivalent transporting capacity of 100 tankers is estimated at 200,000 tons.[14]

The Persian Gulf has become a factor in our domestic oil picture much more quickly than had been anticipated because of the unprecedented demands for petroleum in the United States. Latest plans call for the importation of 100,000 barrels a day to the East Coast by the end of 1948,[15] and it is not unlikely that Arabian oil will be called on in the near future to relieve the impending shortages on the West Coast.

13. Arabian-American Oil Co., *Arabian Oil and World Oil Needs*, p. 19.
14. *Arabian Oil and World Oil Needs*, pp. 43ff.
15. New York *Herald Tribune*, Sept. 8, 1948, p. 34.

The issue of conserving Western Hemisphere, and especially United States, oil resources for a possible emergency is still unsettled. A report by Wallace Pratt to the National Security Resources Board, as yet unpublished, is said to recommend cutting our domestic production 20 per cent under the Maximum Efficient Rate and importing the difference.[16] Such a program might result in supplying a fifth of all our oil requirements from the Middle East. Despite their vulnerability in time of war, Arabian sources might in this way provide a breathing space for the domestic industry to build up its reserves to a safer level.

16. Reported in the *Oil and Gas Journal*, Sept. 30, 1948, p. 48.

APPENDICES

APPENDIX I

INTERNATIONAL PETROLEUM ECONOMICS[1]

Many of the conclusions which we have presented in the body of this study have depended upon an economic analysis of the petroleum industry in its international aspects. Since it would have led us rather far afield to insert an extended discussion of this general topic in the course of our main argument, we have reserved it for an appendix. Without such an examination, however, the conclusions and recommendations which we have made would rest on rather unsubstantial ground.

Two broad economic problems underlie much of the study which we have presented. First, what economic and technological factors explain the structure of the petroleum industry and its economic behaviour? And, secondly, what are the economic aims which any oil policy *might* usefully seek to accomplish? The fact that significant aspects of both these problems are commonly overlooked in almost all discussion of the petroleum industry makes it doubly important to analyze them carefully.

The interrelation of such factors as the following must be considered: the level and stability of prices, the form of industrial organization, technological progress, the location of refineries, the economies of large scale operations, etc. An inquiry which only considers some of these elements may easily arrive at policy prescriptions which do more harm than good. Since most discussions of the industry have only con-

[1]. This study was written by Mr. Chenery who assumes entire responsibility for its content. He is indebted to Professor Edward S. Mason, Mr. Paul Clark, and Mr. A. S. Manne of Harvard University for helpful criticism.

sidered its conservation and monopoly aspects, it is not surprising that they have produced widely varying suggestions. Recently, however, two careful investigations by economists familiar with the industry (but not employed by it) have gone far to bring out the more fundamental problems.[2] It is significant that both these analyses suggest a much more limited field for desirable changes than had earlier writers.

The technology of the production and processing of oil and the nature of its use are important determinants of the structure of the petroleum industry. We will therefore discuss the conditions of supply and demand before considering the organization of the oil companies and the working of the market.

A. THE CONDITIONS OF SUPPLY

The international petroleum trade is based on the movements of oil from the surplus producing areas, which are almost entirely in the tropics and subtropics of the Northern Hemisphere, to the large population centers in the middle latitudes of both hemispheres. The average distance which petroleum moves is some 2,000 miles or more, and transport costs are a dominant factor in the supply problem. This extended movement gives a wide latitude for location of refineries, a problem which is complicated by nationalistic practices as we have seen. The present analysis will consider the economic characteristics of each stage in the supply process from exploration to wholesale distribution; retailing is left out of account as being primarily a domestic problem.

1. THE RELATIVE IMPORTANCE OF EACH STAGE

One significant measure of the relative importance of each stage in the productive process is the capital invested in it. For U.S. companies the following estimates of capital invested are available (in millions of dollars):

2. P. H. Frankel, *Essentials of Petroleum*, London, 1946, and J. S. Bain, *The Economics of the Pacific Coast Petroleum Industry*, Berkeley, 1945-47 (3 Vols.). A different view is presented by E. V. Roscow, *A National Policy for the Oil Industry*, New Haven, 1948.

Table 1

ESTIMATES OF CAPITAL INVESTED BY UNITED STATES COMPANIES

Division	Domestic Investment *		Net Foreign Assets †	
	(1937)	%	(1939)	%
Production and exploration	$ 6,490	45	580	41
Transportation (pipe line only)	1,100	8	90	6
Refining	3,720	25	210	15
Marketing	3,210	22	550	38
Total	14,520		1,430	

* Pogue, *Economics of the Petroleum Industry*, estimates for 1937.
† *American Petroleum Interests in Foreign Countries*, p. 162.

While these two estimates are neither complete nor strictly comparable, they give an idea of the relative size of the investment in each division of the industry. Tanker investment should be added to make the summary more complete.

2. THE ECONOMIES OF SCALE

One of the keys to the understanding of any integrated industry is a knowledge of the phases of the operation which are conducted more efficiently on a large scale.[3] In this respect international industries may differ considerably from their national counterparts because of the differences in risk involved.

In the United States the economies of scale in the petroleum industry are confined to the refining and transportation divisions. Exploration and drilling can be efficiently con-

---

3. See J. M. Clark, *Studies in the Economics of Overhead Costs*, Chap. VI. Economies of scale may be classified as technical, managerial, financial, marketing, and risk reducing. We must also distinguish between the firm and the individual plant, and between volume of output (which is the usual meaning of "scale") and the number of processes or "depth" which are integrated into one firm. The latter will be discussed under vertical integration.

ducted by fairly small companies, as is shown by the large number of "independent" producers who find about half of the new reserves each year.[4] Much of the actual exploration and drilling is done by specialized contractors whose services are available to large and small producers alike. However, many of the independent producers prefer to sell their crude reserves to the major companies, rather than hold them, so that the 20 largest producers own some 65 per cent of the proven reserves in the U.S.[5]

In foreign production the situation is quite different. Here economies of scale in development and production come from three sources. The technological problems are considerably increased by the generally inaccessible country in which oil is found. Concessions are usually granted in larger blocks than in the U.S., so that more capital is required to finance them. Most important, however, is the risk factor. While the chance of finding oil per acre explored outside the U.S. may be as good or better in the long run, it is much less accurately calculable than in the United States [6] because much less geological exploration has been done. The principles of insurance indicate that under such conditions development can be better undertaken by large operators who can diversify their risks by operating in several areas and several countries. This procedure has the added advantage of diversifying the political risk, of which several examples have already been given. In foreign production, then, technical, financial, and risk-reducing economies all favor large firms.

The economies of pipe-line transportation and refining can best be discussed together. No successful "common carrier"

4. The activity of independent producers is at present stimulated considerably by the federal income tax laws. The special treatment provided for prospecting expenses and development of reserves is a substantial incentive to individuals and corporations having taxable income to engage in this activity who would not do so otherwise.

5. *T.N.E.C. Hearings* (A.P.I. edition), p. 518. The percentage has been fairly constant for the past twenty years or so. See *World Petroleum*, Dec. 1947, p. 58.

6. In the United States, about one "wildcat" well (i.e. a well in new territory) in eight discovers oil.

pipe line has ever been operated in the U.S. so far as is known.[7] Very few lines have been built by producers who were not also refiners. Of the existing pipe lines in the U.S., 90 per cent are owned by refiners and the rest were divorced from the old Standard Oil Co. in 1911.[8] Practically all foreign pipe lines are owned by refiners. The reason for this situation is not hard to find. Since almost all the costs of pipe-line operation except fuel costs are fixed, the cost of transporting a barrel of oil at 50 per cent load factor is 50 per cent greater than at 100 per cent.[9] Load factor then becomes the primary consideration, and only operators of large refineries (or several operators in combination) have been willing to take the long-term risk involved in constructing large pipe lines.

The technical economies of large scale pipe-line transmission are very marked. Although all unit costs decrease somewhat with increasing size, the most significant saving is in steel. The reason is apparent from consideration of the formula for the flow of oil through pipe:[10]

$$Q = KID^4$$

where: Q is the rate of flow
K is a constant depending on the type of oil and conditions of transmission
I is the pressure gradient in the pipe
D is the inside diameter of the pipe.

Since the weight of steel depends only upon the square of the diameter (for any given pressure), this relation gives the weight of steel per unit of capacity for a hypothetical line. (See Table 2 on page 150 for an actual calculation.)

Two conditions must apply to both the production and the market for crude in order for large-scale pipe-line transportation to be feasible: both must be fairly concentrated and

7. *T.N.E.C. Hearings*, p. 319.
8. *Ibid.*, p. 16.
9. See Table 3.
10. This is a simplification of Poiseulle's Formula for laminar flow, which holds for most crude lines.

Table 2

WEIGHT OF STEEL REQUIRED FOR VARIOUS DIAMETERS OF PIPE

Nominal Diameter (inches)	Capacity (b/d)	Tons of Steel Per 1000 b/d of Capacity Per Mile
6	7,700	5.12
8	16,800	3.08
12	50,400	1.73
16	97,800	1.16
20	188,400	0.96
24	310,000	0.75

Source: W. G. Heltzel, "Trends in Pipeline Practices," *Oil and Gas Journal*, September 21, 1946, p. 282. The capacities given here are considerably higher than those for similar diameters in the Middle East because more pumping capacity is used. Here a pressure drop of 12 pounds per square inch per mile is assumed and a distance between stations of 80 miles.

Table 3

ESTIMATED TRANSPORT COSTS FOR VARIOUS LOAD FACTORS: "BIG INCH" 24-INCH CRUDE OIL LINE, TEXAS TO NEW YORK *

Daily Throughput (B/D)	300,000	250,000	200,000	150,000
Costs ($1,000 per Year)				
1. Management	870	870	870	870
2. Operation and Maintenance	2,800	2,800	2,800	2,800
3. Electric Power	5,440	3,610	2,490	1,920
4. Taxes	1,610	1,520	1,470	1,450
5. Interest & Depreciation *	3,300	3,300	3,300	3,300
* (Dep. @ 3¼% on $60,000,000) Total	14,020	12,100	10,930	10,340
Cents per Barrel	12.8	13.3	15.0	18.9

* Source: T. E. Swigert, quoted in *The Petroleum Data Book*, 1947, p. H-30.

fairly stable in order to warrant the large investment required. In some cases, however, the competitive advantages of pipe lines are so great that it is economical to build them even if they must be depreciated over a period as short as five years.[11] For isolated fields there is no alternative.

The economies of large-scale pipe-line transportation are just beginning to be realized. Before the war few crude lines larger than sixteen inches had been built. Compared to the 6- to 10-inch line commonly used, water transportation is considerably cheaper. Comparison of the cost per mile, however, is usually misleading because the water route is invariably longer than a direct pipe line. The 24-inch wartime "Big Inch" line from Texas to New Jersey was competitive with the tanker route, which is almost double the land distance. The cost of transport by the smaller lines commonly used, however, is perhaps three times as much per ton-mile as by tanker.[12] Lines as large as the proposed middle eastern lines require little distance advantage to compete with tankers if they can be fully loaded.

While pipe lines can with considerable justice be called "plant facilities" or appendages of refineries, the tanker has more in common with less specialized carriers. Until recently the standard modern tanker has been the T-2, with a capacity of 115,000 barrels. Recently a 200,000 barrel tanker has been put into operation, with a reported reduction in cost of 20 per cent. For a twenty-day round trip voyage this capacity is the equivalent of a 10,000-barrel pipe line. The problems of load factor become similar for the two types of transport as the tanker becomes larger. The effects of both on industrial organization will be discussed below.

11. The average rate of return on a depreciated investment base of all pipe lines in the U.S. was reported to the T.N.E.C. as 28 per cent (*Hearings*, p. 90). On the Interstate Commerce Commission valuations this rate of return was 14 per cent.
12. A variety of comparisons is given in the T.N.E.C. hearings, which show a wide range of variation due to the neglect of scale, load factors, etc. in the computation. In addition, price bears a rather arbitrary relation to cost in the case of an integrated company.

APPENDICES

Although comparisons of average transport rates are subject to many qualifications, as indicated above, the following prewar rates are widely quoted as indicating the relative costs of the three principal methods of transport:

TABLE 4

COST OF CRUDE OIL TRANSPORTATION PER TON-MILE *

Tanker	1.25	mills
Pipe line	3.20	"
Railroad	8.30	"

* J. E. Pogue, *Economics of the Petroleum Industry*, 1939, p. 35, quoted in *T.N.E.C. Hearings*, A.P.I. ed., p. 317.

The economic characteristics of refineries are very similar to those of pipe lines. The economies of scale are not so pronounced for a given composition of output, but the gain in flexibility which accompanies more complete refining units is of great importance in maintaining fuller capacity operation. The importance of overhead costs is shown in Table 5.

TABLE 5

DIRECT COST OF REFINING
(cents per barrel) *

1. Depreciation and obsolescence	12.0
2. Royalty on cracking process	7.0
3. Maintenance	1.5
4. Treating	0.8
5. Plant fuel	9.0
6. Labor	5.7
Total (exclusive of taxes and other fixed charges)	36.0

* Adapted from data in W. Nelson, *Petroleum Refinery Engineering*, New York, 1936. The costs quoted apply to mid-continent crude in 1932.

A somewhat different breakdown of costs is given in the following estimates of the cost of operation of refineries of three different sizes, each of latest prewar design. The fixed costs appear lower because of the exclusion of royalty payments and the low depreciation rate used. Each of these sizes is roughly representative of about a third of U.S. refining capacity.[13]

TABLE 6
TYPICAL PREWAR REFINERY COSTS IN THE UNITED STATES

Size	5,000 b/d	15,000	60,000
Capital Investment	$2,000,000	$5,000,000	$15,000,000
Operating Expenses: (per barrel)			
(1) Fixed Charges	.04	.035	.03
(2) Depreciation (at 7%)	.077	.064	.051
(3) Direct Operation	.16	.11	.08
(4) Miscellaneous	.06	.05	.04
Total cost per barrel of crude refined	.337	.259	.201

* R. E. Wilson, *T.N.E.C. Hearings*, Vol. 15, p. 3861; typical depreciation rates for refineries are higher than that given here.

The cost of refining in the largest refinery is 40 per cent less than in the smallest, but this difference amounts to less than half a cent a gallon of refined products. The computation does not take into account the much greater flexibility of the large-scale plant in the composition of its products. The addition of the newer processes, such as catalytic cracking and polymerization, raises the investment per barrel of throughput but also raises the gasoline yield.

The effect of load factor is as decisive in determining costs in the refining division as in pipe-line transportation. All costs listed in Tables 5 and 6 are inflexible for *any* rate of operation except fuel and a small part of depreciation. Only the largest refineries can shut down one unit without hampering the operations of other units. Likewise the losses in off-grade products due to starting up and shutting down units are considerable, so that refiners are usually faced with a choice of continuous operation or shutting down for long periods.

13. Bain found that relative refining costs in California corresponded roughly to that indicated here although there was considerable variation. *Op. cit.*, Vol. 1, Chap. 5.

Both refining and transportation by pipe line show very marked economies of scale. Together they typically account for about half of the wholesale price of petroleum products. Although the increase in efficiency due to large refineries alone is not a decisive competitive advantage, the combination of large pipe lines with large refineries, which can only exist in combination, is a determining factor in the organization of the petroleum industry. These two stages are inextricably linked by the economic necessity of operating both pipe lines and refineries at a high load factor. This fact is usually overlooked by those who advocate separate ownership of the two.

3. CAPITAL INTENSITY AND THE NEED FOR STABILITY

A factor closely related to overhead costs is capital intensity, which indicates the contribution of capital costs to the total costs of production. Overhead costs include all operating expenses which do not vary with the rate of output. Unlike interest and depreciation, however, *other* overhead costs can be avoided by ceasing operations entirely. The effect of a high degree of capital intensity is to increase the length of time which the firm must plan ahead or to raise the profit margin required.

A rough measure of capital intensity is the ratio of total investment to annual wages.[14] Using the data in Table 1, the capital intensities of the several divisions by this measure are found in Table 7 on page 155. Typical ratios in manufacturing are less than five to one; ratios in petroleum are among the highest of any industry.

Characteristic of the increase in scale of operations in all industries is the accompanying increase in capital intensity due to the introduction of more specialized machinery. In petroleum refining, fuel costs are greater than labor costs except in areas where fuel is very cheap. Increasing size and efficiency

---

14. The commonly used ratio of investment per worker leaves out of account differences in wage rates. A more accurate measure would be the ratio of investment to all direct costs (or to value added in each stage).

TABLE 7

CAPITAL INTENSITY IN UNITED STATES PETROLEUM INDUSTRY

Division	Annual Wages * (Millions)	Investments * (Millions)	Ratio of Investment to Wages
Exploration & production	232	$6,493	28
Pipe line transport	50	$1,104	22
Refining	165	$3,718	22.5
Marketing	559	$3,210	5.7

* Source: J. E. Pogue, *op. cit.*, p. 37 (data for 1937).

results in a substitution of capital equipment for both labor and fuel. This trend is roughly shown in Table 6. The same phenomenon of increasing capital intensity with increasing scale of operations is evident in production, pipe lines, and tankers. In production it is largely a matter of choice. The larger companies hold more reserves per barrel of oil produced than do the smaller ones because their operations are oriented further into the future—i.e. their "time horizon" is longer.[15]

The increase in investment per unit of output as size increases has made the big companies look further into the future in planning their operations. Their greater vulnerability to variations in output is partially offset by the greater stability of a wider market. Since a drop in output will raise their costs more proportionately than in almost any other industry, market sharing and other methods of assuring a stable rate of output are particularly attractive to the international oil companies.[16]

15. At the present time, the thirty largest U.S. producers are producing their reserves at a rate of 6 per cent per year, compared to 10.3 per cent for the rest. *World Oil*, December 1947, p. 58. Part of this difference is due to methods of proration.

16. For a discussion of this point, see Bain, *op. cit.*, Vol. 1, pp. 100-2.

4. THE ELASTICITY OF SUPPLY

One of the most important characteristics of an industry is its response to changes in the price of its products. If the quantity offered for sale is inelastic—i. e. if the percentage change in quantity is less than the percentage change in price—price will fluctuate more than if the supply were elastic. In a competitive market industries which have a large proportion of overhead costs almost invariably have an inelastic supply in the short run: price drops are ineffective in reducing the quantity produced. Over a longer period, the capital intensity and durability of the plant determine the ability of supply to adapt itself to price changes.

Petroleum supplies tend to be inelastic in both the short and long run. Other products, such as minerals and rubber, which require a large specialized investment also have an inelastic supply. The time lag between exploration and production of oil accentuates this lack of sensitivity to price changes, as does a similar production lag in agricultural commodities. The history of U.S. exploration and development shows that changes in the number of wells drilled annually were roughly proportionate to price changes, but the lag in production and the variability of discovery make the correlation between quantity produced and price very poor. The unpredictability of oil discoveries is probably the most disturbing factor to the domestic oil industry, augmented as it is by the "law of capture." It is hard to make any generalizations about the elasticity of the supply of crude in the international market, as it is dominated by a few large corporations. Since they have a longer "time horizon," they may be more sensitive to price changes than is the domestic market. Governmental policies are also a large factor in determining the quantity of oil entering international trade.

The effect of the technological characteristics of transportation and refining—extremely specialized equipment, economies of scale, and large overhead costs—is to accentuate the

APPENDICES   157

inelasticity of supply characteristic of the crude market, particularly in the case of a drop in demand. In the absence of some sort of market control, prices tend to drop toward prime costs for each stage in the productive process. In reality, however, this type of market behaviour has only been apparent in the U.S. market before the Interstate Oil Compact of 1935 and during the early price wars in the international market.

Recent developments in petroleum refining have counteracted somewhat the inelasticity of the supply of *individual* refined products. The effect of increases in the size and diversity of refineries has been to make it easier to vary the proportions of the principle products which are produced. Therefore a drop in the demand for one product can more easily produce a shift to production of another. This "technical substitutability" of joint products of the refining process may become a very important factor in stabilizing the oil industry in conjunction with the growing diversity of demand (to be discussed below).

B. THE DEMAND FOR PETROLEUM PRODUCTS

The rapid rise in petroleum use which has characterized the period since 1913 has been paralleled by a continuous diversification of petroleum products and their uses. In some of these uses petroleum has no substitutes over a considerable price range, while in others it is very competitive with other fuels. A discussion of the demand for petroleum must begin with a classification of uses according to their economic characteristics.

1. NON-COMPETITIVE USES

The two sources of demand for petroleum which caused its rapid development are those in which it has had no close substitutes: gasoline and lubricants. Only a continued rise in the price of crude oil will cause any appreciable substitution of other raw materials in their production (except in the United States, where natural gas is already being used for synthesis). Countries such as Germany which have tried to stimulate the production of synthetic gasoline from coal have found it necessary to double the price of gasoline.

In the short run the demand for these two products is very inelastic. Both of them together constitute only a part of the cost of operation of a motor vehicle—perhaps a third in the United States. Short-term fluctuations in price have little effect upon the consumption of such "auxiliary" commodities. Where the price of gasoline is high, however, it is a larger part of the total cost of vehicle use, and demand may become more elastic.[17] No satisfactory studies of demand have been made, however, and the steady downward trend of gasoline prices in the U.S. until recently affords little opportunity for such a study.

2. COMPETITIVE USES

Until quite recently, gasoline and lubricants were considered the "cash crop" of the refinery, and other products were produced and sold chiefly as by-products at whatever price was necessary to compete with other fuels. Now, however, the demand for intermediate refinery products—diesel fuel and fuel oils—is increasing rapidly. Since these "middle distillates" are also used as the raw material for further refining (cracking) in the production of gasoline, increased substitution of these products for each other is possible.

The diesel engine is replacing steam engines in many uses. Petroleum products have a unique advantage in the transportation field because they contain some 70 per cent more heating value per pound than coal and can be handled and

---

17. Examples of both these tendencies may be cited. In the United States, prices ranged from 13 to 24 cents per gallon in different areas in 1939, but per capita consumption showed no apparent correlation with price after the effects of varying income had been removed. In Turkey, on the other hand, a reduction in price from 75 to 53 cents a gallon caused an increase in consumption of 92 per cent over a 2½-year period (1937-39). The demand in this case was elastic even after allowance is made for secular trend. See *Petroleum Interests in Foreign Countries*, pp. 118, 416.

burned more efficiently. Diesels are already supreme in ocean transport and are rapidly replacing steam engines in railroad locomotives.[18]

Petroleum finds its strongest competition from coal in the heating field. The demand for fuel oil for domestic heating is increasing very rapidly in the U.S., while the heavier residual oils are used like coal for boiler fuel, etc. While oil has the advantage of ease of handling in all uses, the rise in price of other petroleum products may cause a decline in the use of petroleum for heating because of the possibility of producing a greater proportion of the more valuable products in the refining process. From the point of view of rational allocation of world fuel resources, this would seem to be a desirable trend. Coal is used to best advantage in large installations as a source of steam and electric power, and only in cases of long distances from coal supplies can oil displace it in these uses.

Factors other than the relative prices of coal and oil influence their competitive position. The dependability of supply is an important consideration in determining which type of fuel-burning equipment will be installed. Some countries have expressed an unwillingness to become dependent upon an uncertain world petroleum market and have preferred to develop more expensive coal or water power as a basic source of power. In areas where coal is scarce, however, such as Africa and South America, oil replaces coal in almost all

---

18. The following table shows the principal uses of diesel power in the U. S.:

	Installed Horsepower	
Industry	15	Million
Tractors and construction	8	
Railroads	5	
Marine	3.7	
Municipal power plants	2.5	
Trucks	1.9	
Other	5	
Total	41.1	Million

Source: *Oil and Gas Journal*, September 20, 1947, p. 163.

uses; 70 per cent of petroleum consumption in these continents consists of fuel oil.

Where both oil and coal are available in dependable quantities, the relative increase in oil consumption due to a rise in the price of coal [19] is quite high. Many large users maintain stand-by equipment so that they can shift easily from one fuel to the other. This is the only market in which the short-run demand for petroleum is elastic. The trend of wage rates may play an important part in the competition between oil and coal. Since oil requires much less use of labor at each stage, its relative advantage over coal in all uses increases when wage rates rise relative to capital costs. Oil is thus of the greatest importance to the wealthier industrial countries where wage rates are highest.

3. THE EFFECT OF INCOME ON PETROLEUM USE

The use of petroleum throughout the world shows a wide range of variation, from a per capita consumption of 3 gallons a year in the Far East to nearly 600 in the U.S. Most of this variation can be explained by the differences in incomes of the different countries more than by differences in prices of petroleum. If we confine our examination to the more valuable petroleum products, the correlation between per capita income and consumption is very high. In gasoline consumption this relationship is not modified by either distance from source of supplies or availability of coal. Only population density, which determines the efficiency of various forms of transportation, shows any marked effect upon the gasoline consumption in different countries. Any forecast of future demand, therefore, depends predominantly upon a forecast of levels of world prosperity. As a source of fuel and power, the use of petroleum is as much a cause as a result of rising income, however. The increasing availability of adequate petroleum supplies must be considered a major factor in international welfare.

19. Technically, the cross-elasticity of demand.

4. TRENDS IN PETROLEUM CONSUMPTION

The growth in petroleum consumption has come chiefly from the development of new uses rather than from changes in the price of petroleum products. Since petroleum in almost all its uses is an auxiliary commodity, the chief demand for it depends upon the development of oil-burning motors and furnaces and the replacement of other equipment by them. Both these processes take time and account for the short run inelasticity of demand.

There is ample evidence that the thirty years since World War I have not been long enough for world demand to adapt itself to this new fuel. Even allowing for the effect of increasing real income throughout the world, there has been a steady upward trend in consumption in all countries. The trend in the U.S., which had a considerable head start, has been for consumption to double every seventeen years. Foreign consumption has tended to double every thirteen years; the Eastern Hemisphere is slowly making up for its lower consumption by increasing at a more rapid rate than the West. These trends have been unaffected in the Western Hemisphere by the war, while Eastern Hemisphere consumption is perhaps half a million barrels a day (20 per cent) less than it would have been if the war had not intervened. In considering the structure of the petroleum industry it is very important to remember the steady upward demand upon which it has been able to rely.

C. THE ORGANIZATION OF THE INDUSTRY

The analysis of the conditions of supply and demand has been undertaken primarily to shed light on one of the most controversial of industrial questions: the organization of the petroleum industry. Since the formation of the Standard Oil Company, the question of the advantages of integration versus the evils of monopoly has been debated at great length and without conclusive result. The significant fact is that the structure of the industry has remained fundamentally the same ever since international marketing began. The logic of the pattern is determined largely by the technological and economic factors which we have already discussed, and which we shall now endeavor to bring together. The necessity of such a structure can thus be discussed.

1. PATTERNS OF INTEGRATION

The petroleum industry is characterised by both horizontal and vertical combinations. The causes of the former have been frequently discussed by economists,[20] but the analysis of vertical integration is not so clear. Both phenomena are intimately connected with the increasing size of industrial operations resulting from economies of scale. Both types may lead to monopolistic power, which is often the direct aim of large horizontal combinations, but both may have economic justification.

a) *Horizontal Combination*

Combinations among producers of the same products may be formed either to achieve economies of larger scale operation or to obtain a monopolistic position in the market. The former reasons may be given to conceal the monopolistic aim. Various economies of scale are possible. Operating many plants together may permit further specialization and the operation of some plants at full capacity while fluctuations in demand are taken up by a few. While managerial diseconomies are likely to outweigh gains in managerial efficiency, there are real financial economies associated with very large units. In the case of differentiated products, larger output may permit economies of distribution and marketing.

The desire to restrict competition by horizontal combination often comes from the natural instability of the market. The ineffectiveness of the price mechanism in adjusting supply to

20. Notably R. Liefmann in Germany and J. M. Clark in the U.S.

demand may result from either an inelastic supply or an inelastic demand, providing the other is not too elastic.[21]

The commonest causes of an inelastic supply over a period of several years or more are either specialized resources which cannot be readily devoted to alternative uses—such as minerals and some agricultural lands—or large capital investments in specialized equipment. These two categories contain most of the industries which have been characterized by large-scale combinations: tin, rubber, coffee, pig iron, coal, etc. An inelastic demand will of course accentuate the variability of prices.

There are two requirements for successful cartels or other forms of monopolistic combination. Entrance to the industry must be difficult and the product must be fairly standardized. Therefore horizontal combinations have flourished chiefly in raw materials and basic commodities subject to economies of scale. Lacking either of these characteristics, the restriction of supply is not feasible. Given such an industry, however, combination is usually precipitated by unexpected variations in either supply or demand. The latter usually is caused by business depressions; it is well established that the trust movement is stimulated by excess capacity. Unexpected variations in supply, such as the discovery of new resources, may have the same effect however. The discovery of the east Texas oil field at about the time of the great depression is a notable example of both these influences at work, leading to a movement for control of output both in the U.S. and abroad.

In practice it is very difficult to distinguish between combinations motivated primarily by monopolistic aims and those which secure socially desirable economies of scale. While it has been the general consensus among economists that most of the profits obtained by large combinations were due to their monopoly position, it does not seem possible to make valid

21. Technically speaking, the sum of the elasticities of demand and supply at any price determines the amount which price must change to offset a shift in the demand or supply schedules.

generalizations in this field. Each case must be examined on its merits.

b) *Vertical Integration*

The need to extend control over several stages in a single productive process also begins with economies of scale. Since overhead costs usually rise as the size of plants and firms increases, the cost of production depends largely on the level of operation. In such conditions the firm is more vulnerable to stoppages in its supply of raw material or monopolistic practices on the part of its suppliers. Horizontal combinations at any stage are likely to provoke vertical integration [22] as a defensive measure. The steel and oil industries may both be cited in this connection.

Several factors may contribute to the particularly heavy dependence of firms in one stage of production upon those in either earlier or later stages. Specialized methods of transportation limit the capacity of firms providing transport to the demand of one industry and make the supply much less elastic than it is for products moving by less specialized techniques. This has been a very potent factor in the integration of the meat packing, petroleum, gas, electric, and other industries. Extreme specialization of manufacturing equipment has the same effect; the plant has little value except in the processing of one raw material or the making of one product. It is at the mercy of either its suppliers or its marketers or both. High consumption of one or two raw materials relative to the value of the product adds to the pattern of interdependence. This is typically the case of the first stage in processing. The plant may be located at some distance from the source of supply, but it is utterly dependent upon the competitive functioning of that market. Firms utilizing many raw materials can survive the monopolization of one of them, but the advantage of an integrated firm is too great where a large part of total cost consists of one or two raw materials.

22. This point is well discussed by A. R. Burns, *The Decline of Competition*, New York, 1936, Chap. 9.

As a result, unintegrated refiners of minerals and agricultural products are only likely to maintain their position as long as the raw material market is substantially competitive.[23]

A final cause of vertical integration is capital intensity, which determines the length of time over which production must be planned. If it is a characteristic of only one stage, it may lead to horizontal rather than vertical integration as a means of reducing the risk involved. The natural rubber industry with its seven-year planning period is a good case in point. Where large-scale, highly specialized operations are required at another stage in the process, however, the advantages of combined planning become very important.

It is well to note at this point the factors making for vertical disintegration. Primary among them is the unwieldiness of large organizations. Only in the case of one or two very important raw materials is it worth while to try to extend control into an entirely new field. This fact probably accounts for the lack of integration in the automobile industry. The differences in optimum scale of different stages in the productive process usually determine the extent to which vertical integration is carried. Many specialized goods and services are most efficiently provided on a scale larger than any single firm requires. Only if the monopoly profits of the supplier exceed the economies of scale will it pay the manufacturer to supply them himself. In every integrated industry there is usually one central process which shows marked economies of scale, and control is extended forward or backward from it as far as is necessary to secure its optimum operation. Further extension may serve to improve the monopoly position of the firm but it is not likely to lower its costs.

Given an industry susceptible to vertical integration, there are two distinct periods when the opportunity is particularly attractive. When times are good and supplies are scarce, the

23. This is true so long as there is an opportunity for refiners to secure a share of raw material ownership. If the raw material is completely monopolized, independent refiners may continue to exist because the price is kept high enough to allow them a profit.

monopoly position of suppliers is strengthened and "backward" integration to the source of supply becomes profitable. Conversely, when times are bad and demand contracts, there is a strong impulse to extend control forward to the marketing division in order to get distributors who will push the particular firm's product. This tendency leads to differentiation of products which are physically almost indistinguishable. These vertical alignments persist after the need for them has passed although they sometimes break down when the opposite phase of the business cycle is reached.

Although generalizations in this field are dangerous, there seem to be more important possibilities for economy through vertical integration than through horizontal combination. Vertical integration leads to monopoly only if the optimum scale at some stage in the process is so great that it is incompatible with effective competition. The effect of vertical integration on competition is largely a question of the size of the market. In small countries, most vertically integrated firms are likely to have monopoly power, while in large markets there is room for considerable integration without *necessarily* involving monopoly. The size of the firm is a poor test of its monopolistic power unless it is related to the size of the market in which it operates. Vertical integration by itself does not reduce the risk of market fluctuations of the final product because the profitability of all divisions depend upon the volume of the final stage to larger degree than do the profits of an unintegrated firm. For this reason a certain amount of horizontal combination is desirable to spread the market risk if possible.

2. INTEGRATION IN THE PETROLEUM INDUSTRY

The petroleum industry contains almost all the factors which have led to both horizontal and vertical integration in other industries. It can well be argued that if Rockefeller and Deterding had not integrated the industry, some one else would have done so within a short space of time. The process of integration in the petroleum industry is best understood by considering the different routes taken by Standard Oil and Shell in achieving their preeminence.[24] The pattern has not changed much since then.

The old Standard Oil Company is usually taken as the prototype of the integrated oil company in its "unrestricted" form. Its technique of organization consisted of concentration on the bottleneck of the industry, transportation, where economies of scale are pronounced and entry difficult because of the large investment required. The pipe line is better adapted to this technique than either the tanker or the tank car because it is more capital-intensive and yields the greatest economies of scale of all. The development of the pipe line served the purposes of control better than the railroad because it could be owned outright. However, Standard undoubtedly provided a service to the public by building pipe lines, whose economy over railroad transport is unquestioned. The economies of large-scale refining played a lesser part in the early organization of the industry although continuity of operation probably was an important factor. Standard stayed out of the field of production to a large extent because so long as it remained competitive the other divisions were more profitable. Horizontal integration was carried much further than vertical integration in this early period.

The problems of Shell in the international field were different from those of the domestic U.S. market, and Deterding's solution of them was better than Standard's. In the world market crude moves a much longer distance than it does in any country which has indigenous supplies. The tanker is a more flexible instrument than the pipe line, and so diversity of supplies is more important in reducing costs than control of any other branch. Deterding's cardinal principle was to supply each market from a source of crude as close to it as possible. This aim made the development of geographically diversified fields of primary importance. Once Shell's position was established, it became more and more favorable as U.S.

24. Frankel, *op. cit.*, Part IV, gives a very illuminating analysis of this process.

production costs rose compared to the rest of the world. Standard was forced to play the same game of searching for oil in all parts of the world in order to maintain its position in the world market. Integration was therefore extended one step backward to the source of supply, and the future pattern of the world petroleum trade was fixed. Firms without varied sources of oil have never played a very great part in it. The large optimum scale of operations in the productive branch has chiefly determined the size of operations in subsequent stages. It is significant that the largest refineries, the largest pipe lines, and the largest tankers are all being used outside the U.S. The large units of production under one control permit "rationalization" of the rest of the industry to be carried much further. But the inevitable result is the reduction of the number of firms and the formation of an oligopoly—the domination of the market by a small group.

An interesting corollary of Deterding's technique is the need for close cooperation between producing companies and their governments in securing concessions. In this too, England has taken the lead and the U.S. has followed.

3. THE EFFECT OF NATIONAL POLICIES

While completely "free" competition in the international petroleum field would probably result in a few completely integrated companies, competition is anything but free. The nationalistic policies of both producing and consuming countries have been mentioned. What is their effect upon the world market?

a) *The Supply of Crude*

We have seen that the need for large units in production arises not from technological factors but from the risks involved. If governments assume these risks by hiring independent contractors to conduct exploration and drilling, the effect upon the world market may be salutary. If, as more often happens, they encourage private firms to assume the risk and later expropriate a large part of the profits in the event of success, they raise the overall risk of private exploration and private enterprise is discouraged accordingly. In many cases it is clear that the net effect of the government policy has been harmful to both the country and the private company, and world supplies of oil are reduced.

The policy of producing countries, if not too restrictive, may however go far toward restoring competition to the world market. There are considerably more producing countries than large-scale oil companies, and their number is increasing. Their pressure for royalties may provide the competitive element in the market which might otherwise be missing in some areas.

b) *The Refining of Crude*

The ideal location of refineries is determined by several factors. Petroleum loses so little weight in the refining process that the balance between market location and supply orientation becomes a delicate one. The increased bulk of crude to be transported to a market location must be weighed against the higher cost of transporting products (by tanker or pipe line) and the increased flexibility which the market location has in its choice of crude. Since petroleum moves most by water in international trade, a third possibility is available: the location of refineries at seaboard, either near the market or near the field. These locations may combine the flexibility of choice of crudes with choice of markets.

In practice all three types of location are common. The largest refineries are found at seaboard near the largest oil fields: at Abadan in Iran, Aruba off the Venezuelan coast, and Houston near the Texas fields. They exploit cheap fuel and economies of scale. Their wide choice of markets permits full utilization of refining and transport facilities. Concentrated markets foster the next largest scale of refinery: the U.S. east and west coasts both have several 100,000 b/d refineries near the largest markets.[25] Small refineries usually are located in the oil fields, where fuel economies are not im-

25. A new 120,000 b/d refinery is planned near London, England.

portant, or near smaller markets. Although refineries smaller than 10,000 b/d, and especially those smaller than 5,000 barrels, are inefficient, many of them persist both in this country and abroad.

Two factors prevent the elimination of these uneconomically small units. In the United States they are almost all in the oil fields and were built to operate on cheap crude. Since transportation is a large part of the total cost of petroleum products, a small differential in the distance involved may allow the inefficient unit to be maintained as a marginal producer. Abroad, however, the reason is largely political. Since all crude is imported, high taxes on refined products or licensing control are usually necessary to make foreign companies refine their oil in the uneconomically small refineries required by the small markets in the importing countries. The result of this policy can be seen from a comparison of the American-owned refineries in Canada and Latin America with those in Europe. In the former nearly 90 per cent of American refining capacity consists of units of 10,000 barrels or larger. In Europe only two of the twenty or so American refineries are this large, and their capacity is only 40 per cent of the total. It is probable that few of these refineries would have been built at all without pressure from the importing governments.[26] One cause of high unit costs of these small refineries is the unbalanced output, which may not conform to the demands of the local market for the various petroleum products.

The causes of this insistence upon local refining capacity are ostensibly to stimulate local employment and reduce the demands for foreign exchange, but the desire for self-sufficiency is more important. As long as dollars are scarce, the argument for importing crude instead of refined products from dollar sources has some economic validity.

In summary, we may say that few markets outside the United States are large and diversified enough to make mar-

---

26. *Petroleum Interests in Foreign Countries*, p. 204. In the U.S. 80 per cent of the refining capacity consists of units larger than 10,000 b/d.

ket location of refineries advantageous on purely economic grounds. The best location in general is at tidewater near the source of supply. Very small refineries are likely to exist only under government protection except in times of scarcity.

4. MARKET BEHAVIOUR

Price making in the domestic oil industry has been frequently investigated, but little evidence is available on the workings of the international market. We will consider the domestic market first.

From the comprehensive investigations of the Temporary National Economic Committee, a fairly clear-cut classification of geographical price structures can be made, based on the type of products involved.[27] Uniform f.o.b. plant pricing and uniform delivered prices prevail only in industries in which transport costs are a small per cent of the total cost or in which the product is highly differentiated. Standardized commodities for which transport costs are a sizable share of the total cost are usually sold according to some system of freight equalization or basing points in the absence of perfect competition. The existence of a high percentage of overhead costs increases the need for an accepted method of price stabilization to avoid ruinous price wars.

The petroleum industry employs several variations of the latter methods. In the U.S. market there are too many producers and too many sources of supply to permit a basing point system to be consistently maintained, and so prices are set by price leaders most of the time with occasional violent wars when demand is slack. In the international market the price wars have been absent for some time. The Gulf coast has been the only place where there is a quoted price for crude, and it has served as a basing point for the world market. The shortage of crude for export in the U.S. and the growing importance of Venezuela and the Persian Gulf may produce new basing points for the international oil trade.

27. See *T.N.E.C. Monograph No. 1*, pp. 343-44, for a summary of findings.

The basing point system has often been attacked by economists, but it is sometimes difficult to suggest a method which would provide better results. J. M. Clark finds that industries using a basing point system have four characteristics in common: [28]

(1) A standardized commodity
(2) Localized production, with several producing centers
(3) A high percentage of overhead costs
(4) A substantial percentage of costs due to transportation

It is apparent that the petroleum industry fits this category, along with steel, cement, and several other industries. The fewer the producing units, the easier it is for the system to be maintained, which explains its persistence in the international market. So long as the base price yields monopoly profits to lower-cost producers, they are likely to maintain it if their volume is not too greatly restricted. The petroleum industry is particularly suited to this practice because the international companies all produce and sell in several regions and all except Anglo-Iranian are among the largest U.S. producers. So long as world demand continues to expand at a predictable rate they are not likely to be afflicted with excess capacity and will have no incentive to cut prices to a competitive level.

We can criticize the basing point method in the international oil trade only in the light of other (mainly political) considerations. If the Persian Gulf becomes a basing point, as seems quite probable, the European market results would be similar to those under any other form of pricing by the oligopoly, such as local price leadership. The maintenance of the Gulf Coast as a basing point after it no longer provides a substantial share of the world market, however, has already aroused protests in England and is likely to arouse more from the other importing countries.[29]

28. "Basing Point Methods of Price Quoting," *Canadian Journal of Economics and Political Science*, Nov. 1938, Vol. 4, No. 4, pp. 477ff.

29. See Frankel, *op. cit.*, pp. 115-16. See Chap. IX for current discussion of the basing point system.

The producing countries themselves are more likely to provide the effective competitive element in the world petroleum trade than the large companies, once refining and transport capacity have caught up with world demand (five to ten years hence). Until then, competition cannot be much of a factor in any case.

5. CONSERVATION AND TECHNOLOGICAL PROGRESS

It is well known that unregulated competition has worse effects on the conservation of irreplaceable resources than almost any other method of exploitation. Within a national economy it is theoretically possible to preserve competition while effecting conservation (although it has rarely been done effectively). In the absence of a world agreement on the conservation of scarce resources, this alternative is not available for international industries. In a perfectly competitive market, countries which enforced conservation would be likely to lose a large share of their current exports because of the higher costs of production involved. From the long-run point of view it is clear that some system which maintains prices at a level which permits conservation is desirable. This is not yet a problem in the international field because few oil fields are producing at their maximum efficient rate, but it is likely to be increasingly important in the future. Conservation in the U.S. while exports continued has been possible only through the operation of the basing point system and the self-restraint of the large international producers.

The technology of the petroleum industry is as varied and highly developed as that of any industry. Technological progress has proceeded at a very rapid rate. Most developments have been made in the United States, where the industry is quite competitive, and transferred to the international sphere quite promptly since the companies involved are the same. While it is quite likely that complete control of the industry by the oligopoly would slow down the rate of technological development, the present state of competition can hardly be criticized for failing to bring forth new developments. Fairly large organizations are necessary to sustain the large research programs required although the fact that most developments have come from the major companies does not prove that this will continue to be the case. The contrast of oil with the coal industry, in which excessive competition has practically eliminated technological progress in many countries, is striking.

There seems to be no necessary correlation between the form of industrial organization and the rate of technological development except in advanced cases of oligopoly or monopoly. Even in countries where whole industries have been cartelized, such as Germany, there is little evidence that technological development has suffered although the timing of the introduction of new processes doubtless has been controlled.

D. SUMMARY

The purpose of this appendix has been to discuss the economic aspects of petroleum as they affect the interests of the United States and the welfare of the world community. We will sum up the most important results of our inquiry.

The oil industry is unique in that it handles a liquid product from start to finish. As a result, very large and highly specialized units of equipment produce economies at each stage of its operations. Production must be developed in the out-of-the-way parts of the world where oil occurs. The necessity of coordinating the construction and functioning of refineries and oil carriers with far-flung sources of production provides a conclusive argument for integrated operation of these stages in the international oil business. The need for integration is stronger in petroleum than in most other commodities because supplies are more uncertain and the transportation media are peculiar to the industry and hence cannot be shared with other products. For these reasons there are real economies in vertical integration which may be absent in other businesses. When all risks are taken into account, it is doubtful that the number of efficient firms which could exist in the world market would be large enough to bring about competitive pricing in many sectors.

Despite the natural tendency toward control of the market by a few sellers which results from these economies, there are several market elements which may stop oligopoly control from becoming oppressive. First, the number of producing countries is increasing, and their pressure for royalties may prevent any monopolistic restriction in the supply of oil. Secondly, the number of important international oil companies has grown from three to seven and may increase further as the market expands. Even though these companies are involved in various alliances through joint ownership of subsidiaries, the danger of effective cartel restrictions on output decreases as the number of participants grows. It is impossible to say what the optimum number of companies in the industry should be, but we have suggested that there are some advantages in terms of conservation and orderly development in having less than the number required for perfect competition.

The analysis of supply and demand conditions has shown that it is peculiarly difficult for any automatic system to provide optimum results in the pricing, output, and conservation of oil. This fact gives rise to the demands for international controls which we have discussed in Chapter VIII. The importance of oil and the economic nature of the industry which supplies it may require special treatment of this commodity in international trade.

APPENDIX II

STATISTICAL APPENDIX*

Table 1. World Oil Reserves and Ownership

Table 2. World Petroleum Balance Sheet, 1946

Table 3. Interregional Movements of Petroleum, 1946

Table 4. United States Supply and Exports of Petroleum (by years)

Table 5. Middle East Oil Companies

Table 6. Middle East Oil Production (by countries)

Table 7. Petroleum Export-Import Forecast, 1955

Table 8. Middle East Pipe Lines.

* We are indebted to the editors of the *Petroleum Data Book* and the *Oil and Gas Journal* for permission to use material from those sources.

TABLE I WORLD OIL RESERVES AND OWNERSHIP *

	Proved reserves (billion barrels) Jan. 1947	% of world ¶	Producing wells	% Ownership			Estimated production 1947 § (1000 b/d)	Production as % of reserves	Potential at 6% of reserves	Excess potential
				United States	British-Dutch	Other				
United States	21.9	33.2	425,650	98%	2	0	5,275	8.8%	3,600	−1,675
Other North America	1.0	1.5	3,215	} 65	24	11	175	6.4%	160	− 15
South America	8.9	13.5	15,705		27	46	1,410	5.8%	1,460	+ 50
Europe	0.8	1.2	7,185	27	0	100	130	5.9%	130	0
USSR	6.0 †	9.1	11,750	0	100	0	550	3.3%	990	+ 440
Africa	0.1	0.1	195	0	52	6	25	9.0%	15	− 10
Middle East	26.0 ‡	39.4	195	42	73	3	860	1.2%	4,270	+3,410
Far East	1.3	2.0	6,710	24	40	20	65	1.8%	210	+ 145
Total Outside U.S.	44.1	66.8	44,955	40	28	14	3,215	2.8%	7,235	+4,020
Total World	66.0	100.0	470,605	58			8,490	4.7%	10,835	+2,345
Eastern Hemisphere	34.2	52%								
Western Hemisphere	31.8	48%								

* Source: *The Petroleum Data Book*, Petroleum Engineer Publishing Co., 1947.
† Russian reserves are variously estimated up to 10 billion.
‡ Middle East reserves are variously estimated up to 30 billion.
§ Estimated by *Oil and Gas Journal*, December 27, 1947, p. 156.
¶ The figures used in Chapter II are based on an estimate of 30 billion for Middle East reserves.

TABLE 2   WORLD PETROLEUM BALANCE SHEET, 1946 *

	Total † production (thousand b/d)	Inter-Area:			Consumption				1946 Refining capacity
		Imports	Exports	Import balance	1946 ‡	% Increase over 1938	1947 (est.) §	Forecast (1951) ‖	
United States	5070	370	410	−40	4910	58%	5400	6300	5400
Other North America	150	230	0	230	440	70%		600	440
South America	1290	20	860	−840	380	60%		500	990
Western Hemisphere	6510	0	650	−650	5730	59%	6310	7400	6830
Europe	180	680	60	620	810	−13%	1000	1340 (1500)	440
USSR	490	90	0	90	540	−4%	550	900	580
Africa	30	110	0	110	160	+23%		240	30
Middle East	690	0	500	−500	140	+100%		210	740
Far East	30	220	20	200	230	+6%		320	50
Oceania	40	160	10	150	190	+57%		260	70
Eastern Hemisphere	1460	650	0	+650	2070	+25%	2370	3270	1910
Total World	7970				7800	+39%	8680	10670	8740

* Sources: *The Petroleum Data Book*, 1947; *Oil and Gas Journal* (Forecasts).
† Production figures exceed those given in Table 1 by the amount of production from other sources than crude (natural gasoline, benzol, synthetics, etc.).
‡ Consumption figures differ from the total of production plus import balance by the change in stocks in storage.
§ Estimates for 1947 from Bureau of Mines (U.S.), *Oil and Gas Journal*, and CEEC Report (Europe).
‖ Forecast for 1951 based on those of the Standard Oil Co. (N.J.), published in *The Lamp*, September 1947, and the *Oil and Gas Journal*, December 27, 1947, p. 156. (The CEEC forecast for Europe is given in parentheses.)

TABLE 3

INTERREGIONAL MOVEMENTS OF PETROLEUM,* 1946 †

(1000 Barrels per Day)

To:

From:	North America	South America	Europe	USSR	Africa	Middle East	Far East	Oceania	Total Exports	Change from 1938
North America		8	176	9	13	0	15	30	251	−180
South America	427 ‡		381 §	0	41	0	1	9	859	+332
Europe	0	0	2	61	1	0	0	0	62	+40
USSR	0	0			0	0	0	0	2	−20
Africa	0	0	1	0		1	0	0	2	0
Middle East	8	8	125	0	52		189	122	503	+304
Far East (incl. Sakhalin)	0	0	0	18	0	0		0	18	+12
Oceania	0	0	0	0	0	0	15		15	−64
Total Imports ‖	435	16	685	88	107	1	220	161	1712	+424 ¶

* Includes crude oil and products.
† Source: *The Petroleum Data Book*, 1947.
‡ 352 to United States and 75 to Canada.
§ 361 from Caribbean Area.
‖ Not shown in the above analysis: (1) United States to Canada: 130
(2) Caribbean to Latin America: 187

¶ Increase over 1938 is 38%.

TABLE 4

UNITED STATES SUPPLY AND EXPORTS OF PETROLEUM AND NATURAL GASOLINE *

(In thousands of barrels)

Period or year	United States supply			Imports of crude and refined oils ‡	Total supply	Exports of crude and refined oils ‡	Percentage of total supply	
	Production							
	Crude oil	Natural gasoline †					Imported	Exported
Average:								
1901–10	137,426	.....	295 §	137,721	29,777	0.2	21.6
1911–20	305,200	3,550	31,802	340,552	59,093	9.3	17.4
1921–30	771,862	31,114	89,614	892,590	122,713	10.0	13.7
1931–40	1,065,794	44,025	62,048	1,171,867	139,587	5.3	11.9
1941–45	1,537,179	68,926	80,479	1,686,584	153,518	4.8	9.1
1941	1,402,228	64,017	97,142	1,563,387	108,830	6.2	7.0
1942	1,386,645	64,904	35,966	1,487,515	116,907	2.4	7.9
1943	1,505,613	66,029	63,412	1,635,054	149,957	3.9	9.2
1944	1,677,753	72,174	92,256	1,842,183	208,911	5.0	11.3
1945	1,713,655	77,506	113,619	1,904,780	182,983	6.0	9.6
1946 ‖	1,733,424	80,480	135,033	1,948,937	151,204	6.9	7.8
1947	1,856,100	132,700	157,600	2,148,400	164,400	7.4	7.6
1948 ¶	2,014,000	146,000	187,000	2,347,000	142,000	8.0	6.0

* Sources: *United States Petroleum Import Prospects*, Department of Commerce, July, 1947, and Bureau of Mines.
† Natural gasoline is included because it is blended with or sold as a petroleum product; liquefied gases are excluded.
‡ Imports and exports 1901–10 from Department of Commerce; for subsequent years from Bureau of Mines, representing external trade of the continental United States.
§ Average for 1908–10.
‖ Preliminary.
¶ As forecast August, 1948.

TABLE 5 MIDDLE EAST OIL COMPANIES *

Companies	Anglo-Iranian Oil Co.	Iraq Petroleum Co.	Kuwait Oil Co.	Bahrein Petroleum Co.	Arabian-American Oil Co.	Total Middle East
A. *Owners*	British Government 56%	Anglo-Iranian Oil Co. 23.75% Royal Dutch-Shell 23.75%	Anglo-Iranian 50%	Standard Oil Co. of Cal. 50%	Standard of California 30%	
	Burmah Oil Co. 22%	Cie. Francaise des Petroles 23.75%	Gulf Exploration Co. 50%	Texas Co. 50%	Texas Co. 30% Standard of N.J. 30%	
	Public 22%	S.O.N.J. & Socony-Vacuum 23.75% C. S. Gulbenkian 5%			Socony-Vacuum 10%	
B. *Concessions* 1. Size	Iran 100,000 sq. mi.	Iraq. & Qatar 140,000 sq. mi. Oman, Dhotar, Asir, Hejaz, Palestine, Syria, Lebanon, Trans-Jordan } No oil discovered	Kuwait 6000 sq. mi.	Bahrein Islands (entire)	Saudi Arabia 440,000 sq. mi.	
2. Date granted	1901 (Revised 1933)	1925, 1933, 1938 (Iraq)	1934	1930 (Revised 1940)	1933, 1939	
3. Term	99 yrs.	Terms: 75 years	75 yrs.	55 yrs. (1995)	60 yrs. (1999)	
C. *Reserves* (billion barrels)		5–7.5 Iraq				
1. Proven †	7–9 (billion)	1 Qatar	5–9	0.3	6–7	28–32 billion
2. Potential ‡	40	25 –	10		40	115 billion
D. *Production* 1. Commercial production began:	1913	1927	1946	1933	1938	
2. No. of fields	7	6	1	1	5	20 (fields)
3. Producing wells §	72	11	11	67	70	231 (wells)
4. Daily production §	410,000 b/d	97,000	50,000	24,000	280,000	860,000 b/d
5. Total past production (to 1946)	1,604 million barrels	316 million		75	115	2,110
6. Annual production as % of reserves	1.8%	0.7%			1.3%	1.0%
E. *Refining Capacity*	420,000 b/d—Abadan 2,000—Kermanshah	Haifa 90,000 b/d Iraq 10,000		160,000	135,000	817,000 b/d
F. *Proposed Pipelines* 1. Capacity	500,000 b/d	(1) 90,000 b/d (existing) (2) 175,000 b/d 1951 (3) 300,000 b/d 1953	300,000		300,000 b/d	1,665,000 b/d
2. Completion	1952		1953		1950	1953
G. *Royalties* 1. Rate	20.6 cents / bbl.	22 cents	14 cents	14 cents	22 cents	
2. Current payments	$31,000,000	$7,250,000	$2,000,000	$1,275,000	$21,000,000	$62,500,000

* Sources: *Oil and Gas Journal* and *Arabian American Oil Co.* Proven reserves are the range of estimates given for 1947 by various sources.

† Estimates of potential reserves vary widely. These are based on L. S. Thompson, *Mining and Metallurgy*, May, 1946, p. 251.

§ Production rate at end of 1947.

TABLE 6
MIDDLE EAST OIL PRODUCTION BY COUNTRIES [*]
(Average Daily Rate) 1000 b/d

Year	Egypt	Iran	Iraq	Bahrein	Saudi Arabia	Kuwait	Total	% World
1911	0.1						0.1	...
1912	0.6						0.6	0.1%
1913	0.3	5.1					5.4	0.5
1914	2.1	8.0					10.0	0.9
1915	0.6	9.9					10.0	0.9
1916	1.1	12.2					13.0	1.1
1917	2.6	19.6					22.0	1.6
1918	5.3	23.6					29.0	2.1
1919	4.2	27.8					32.0	2.1
1920	2.8	33.4					36.0	1.9
1921	3.4	45.7					49.0	2.3
1922	3.2	61.0					64.0	2.7
1923	2.9	69.1					72.0	2.6
1924	3.1	88.5					92.0	3.3
1925	3.4	96.0					99.0	3.4
1926	3.3	98.2					101.0	3.4
1927	3.5	108.7	0.9				113.0	3.3
1928	5.0	118.7	1.9				126.0	3.5
1929	5.1	115.5	2.2				123.0	3.0
1930	5.5	125.6	2.5				134.0	3.5
1931	5.6	121.6	2.5				130.0	3.4
1932	5.2	135.2	2.3				143.0	4.0
1933	4.6	149.0	2.5	0.1			156.0	4.0
1934	4.2	158.5	21.1	0.8			185.0	4.4
1935	3.6	156.9	75.1	3.5			239.0	5.3
1936	3.5	171.4	83.1	12.7	0.1		271.0	5.5
1937	3.3	213.2	87.2	21.3	0.2		325.0	5.8
1938	4.3	214.7	89.4	22.7	1.4		333.0	6.1
1939	12.8	214.1	84.4	20.8	10.8		343.0	6.0
1940	17.8	180.9	66.2	19.3	14.7		299.0	5.1
1941	23.4	139.0	34.7	18.6	16.1		232.0	3.8
1942	22.4	208.2	47.8	19.5	12.4		310.0	5.5
1943	24.6	208.2	72.0	18.0	15.0		338.0	5.5
1944	24.9	278.7	90.2	18.3	21.3		433.0	6.3
1945	26.0	352.0	95.7	20.0	58.4		552.0	7.7
1946	25.3	400.0	95.7	20.0	162.6	11.7	715.0	9.4
1947	24.0	420.0	96.0	24.0	247.0	50.0	861.0	10.4
1948 (est.)	30	425	50	30	410	100	1045.0	11.5

[*] Sources: *Petroleum Data Book,* 1947 and Arabian-American Oil Co.

TABLE 7

PETROLEUM* EXPORT-IMPORT FORECAST, 1955† (1000 barrels per day)

To:

From:	North America	South America	Europe	USSR	Africa	Middle East	Far East	Oceania	Totals	Change from 1946
North America			30	0	0	0	10	10	50	− 200
South America	1310		40	0	20	0	0	0	1370	+ 510
Europe	0	0		0	0	0	0	0	0	− 60
USSR	0	0	0		0	0	0	0	0	0
Africa	0	0	0	0		0	0	0	0	0
Middle East	190	0	1430	0	250		300	120	2290	+1790
Far East	0	0	0	0	0	0		0	0	− 20
Oceania	0	0	0	0	0	0	10		10	0
Total Imports	1500	0	1500	0	270	0	320	130	3720	+2020
Domestic Production	6300‡	2000	200	1000	50	2540	40	180	12,310	+4340
Exports	50	1370	0	0	0	2290	0	10	3720	+2020
Total Consumption	7750	630	1700	1000	320	250	360	300	12,310	+4500

* Includes all petroleum and synthetic products. † For discussion of assumptions, see Chapters 2 and 3.
‡ Includes 700,000 b/d of natural gasoline, condensates, and synthetic gasoline in the U. S.

Table 8

MIDDLE EAST PIPE LINES *

	Size	Route	Capacity in B/D	Scheduled Completion Date
A. Already Completed				
Iraq Petroleum Co.	12"	Kirkuk/Haifa	43,750	---
" " "	12"	Kirkuk/Tripoli	43,750	---
			87,500	
B. To Be Completed By Mid-1950				
Iraq Petroleum Co.	16"	Kirkuk/Haifa	87,500	1/ 1/49
" " "	16"	Kirkuk/Tripoli	87,500	4/ 1/50
Trans-Arabian P.L. Co.	30"-31"	Arabia/Sidon	300,000 †	6/ 1/50
			475,000	
C. To Be Completed By End 1953				
Middle East P.L. Co.	34"-36"	Iran/Syria	535,000	6/ 1/51
Kuwait Eastern P.L. Co.	34"-36"	Kuwait/?	300,000	1/ 1/53
Iraq Petroleum Co.	30"	Kirkuk/Tripoli	300,000	12/31/53
			1,135,000	
Grand Total			1,697,500	

* Arabian-American Oil Co., "Oil and the Economic Prosperity of the Middle East," p. 4.

† It is planned to eventually increase the capacity of this pipe line to 500,000 b/d by the installation of additional pumping stations.

APPENDIX III

AN AGREEMENT ON PETROLEUM BETWEEN THE GOVERNMENT OF THE UNITED STATES OF AMERICA AND THE GOVERNMENT OF THE UNITED KINGDOM OF GREAT BRITAIN AND NORTHERN IRELAND

(As amended by the Senate Committee on Foreign Relations in its Report dated July 7, 1947)[1]

PREAMBLE.

The Government of the United States of America and the Government of the United Kingdom of Great Britain and Northern Ireland, whose nationals hold, to a substantial extent jointly, rights to explore and develop petroleum resources in other countries, recognize:—

1. That ample supplies of petroleum, available in international trade to meet increasing market demands, are essential for both the security and economic well-being of nations;

2. That for the foreseeable future the petroleum resources of the world are adequate to assure the availability of such supplies;

3. That the prosperity and security of all nations require the efficient and orderly development of the international petroleum trade;

4. That the orderly development of the international petroleum trade can best be promoted by international agreement among all countries interested in the petroleum trade, whether as producers or consumers.

---

[1]. This text shows the clauses of the original text of the agreement, signed by representatives of the United States and the United Kingdom, which have been struck out by the Committee. The Committee's amendments are italicized.

The two Governments have therefore decided, as a preliminary measure to the calling of an international conference to consider the negotiation of a multilateral petroleum agreement, to conclude the following Agreement.

ARTICLE I.

The signatory Governments agree that the international petroleum trade in all its aspects should be conducted in an orderly manner on a world-wide basis with due regard to the considerations set forth in the Preamble, and within the framework of applicable laws and concession contracts. To this end and subject always to considerations of military security and to the provisions of such arrangements for the preservation of peace and prevention of aggression as may be in force the signatory Governments affirm the following general principles with respect to the international petroleum trade:

(a) That adequate supplies of petroleum, which shall in this Agreement mean crude petroleum and its derivatives, should be accessible in international trade to the nationals of all countries on a competitive and nondiscriminatory basis;

(b) That, in making supplies of petroleum thus accessible in international trade, the interests of producing countries should be safeguarded with a view to their economic advancement.

ARTICLE II.

In furtherance of the purposes of this Agreement, the signatory Governments will so direct their efforts:

(a) That all valid concession contracts and lawfully acquired rights shall be respected, and that there shall be no interference directly or indirectly with such contracts or rights;

(b) that with regard to the acquisition of exploration and development rights the principle of equal opportunity shall be respected;

APPENDICES

(c) that the exploration for and development of petroleum resources, the construction and operation of refineries and other facilities, and the distribution of petroleum, shall not be hampered by restrictions inconsistent *with the provisions of sections* (a) *and* (b) *of Article II.*

ARTICLE III.

1. With a view to the wider adoption of the principles embodied in this Agreement, the signatory Governments agree that as soon as practicable they will propose to the governments of all interested producing and consuming countries the negotiations of an International Petroleum Agreement, which *inter alia* would establish a permanent International Petroleum Council.

2. To this end the signatory Governments agree to formulate at an early date plans for an international conference to negotiate such a multilateral petroleum agreement. They will consult together and with other interested governments with a view to taking whatever action is necessary to prepare for the proposed conference.

ARTICLE IV.

1. Numerous problems of joint immediate interest to the signatory Governments with respect to the international petroleum trade should be discussed and resolved on a cooperative interim basis if the general petroleum supply situation is not to deteriorate.

2. With this end in view, the signatory Governments agree to establish an International Petroleum Commission to be composed of six members, three members to be appointed immediately by each Government. To enable the Commission to maintain close contact with the operations of the petroleum industry, the signatory Governments will facilitate full and adequate consultation with their nationals engaged in the petroleum industry.

3. In furtherance of and in accordance with the purposes

of this Agreement, the Commission shall consider problems of mutual interest to the signatory Governments and their nationals, and with a view to the equitable disposition of such problems it shall be charged with the following duties and responsibilities:

(a) To study the problems of the international petroleum trade caused by dislocations resulting from war;

(b) To study past and current trends in the international petroleum trade;

(c) To study the effects of changing technology upon the international petroleum trade;

(d) To prepare periodic estimates of world demands for petroleum and of the supplies available for meeting the demands, and to report as to means by which such demands and supplies may be correlated so as to further the efficient and orderly conduct of the international petroleum trade;

(e) To make such additional reports as may be appropriate for achieving the purposes of this Agreement and for the broader general understanding of the problems of the international petroleum trade.

4. The Commission shall have power to regulate its procedure and shall establish such organization as may be necessary to carry out its functions under this Agreement. The expenses of the Commission shall be shared equally by the signatory Governments.

ARTICLE V.

The signatory Governments agree:

(a) That they will seek to obtain the collaboration of the governments of other producing and consuming countries for the realization of the purposes of this Agreement, and to consult with such governments in connection with activities of the Commission;

(b) That they will assist in making available to the Commission such information as may be required for the discharge of its functions.

ARTICLE VI.

The signatory Governments agree:

(a) That the reports of the Commission shall be published unless in any particular case either Government decides otherwise;

(b) That no provision in this Agreement shall be construed to require either Government to act upon any report or proposal made by the Commission, or to require the nationals of either Government to comply with any report or proposal made by the Commission, whether or not the report or proposal is approved by that Government.

ARTICLE VII.

The signatory Governments agree:

(a) That the general purpose of this Agreement is to facilitate the orderly development of the international petroleum trade, and that no provision in this Agreement, with the exception of Article II, is to be construed as applying to the operation of the domestic petroleum industry within the country of either Government;

(b) That nothing in this Agreement shall be construed as impairing or modifying any law or regulation, or the right to enact any law or regulation, relating to the importation of petroleum into the country of either Government, *or implying any commitment of any kind, not so to act, as either Government in its discretion may see fit, for the purpose of giving adequate protection to its domestic industry;*

(c) That, for the purposes of this Article, the word "country" shall mean

  (i) in relation to the Government of the United Kingdom of Great Britain and Northern Ireland, the United Kingdom, those British colonies, overseas territories, protectorates, protected states, and all mandated territories administered by that Government and

(ii) in relation to the Government of the United States of America, the continental United States and all territory under the jurisdiction of the United States,

lists of which, as of the date of this Agreement, have been exchanged.

ARTICLE VIII.

This Agreement shall enter into force upon a date to be agreed upon after each Government shall have notified the other of its readiness to bring the Agreement into force and shall continue in force until three months after notice of termination has been given by either Government or until it is superseded by the International Petroleum Agreement contemplated in Article III.

In witness whereof the undersigned, duly authorized thereto, have signed this Agreement.

Done in London, in duplicate, this twenty-fourth day of September, one thousand nine hundred and forty five.

For the Government of the United States of America:
HAROLD L. ICKES.

For the Government of the United Kingdom of Great Britain and Northern Ireland:
EMANUEL SHINWELL.

CHARTER OF PETROLEUM RESERVES CORPORATION [1]

Reconstruction Finance Corporation hereby declares:

First, that pursuant to the authority contained in section 5d of the Reconstruction Finance Corporation Act, as amended, at the request of the Secretary of Commerce, with the approval of the President, there has been created a corporation under the name of Petroleum Reserves Corporation (hereinafter referred to as the "Corporation").

1. *Federal Register*, July 2, 1943.

Second, that the location of the principal office of the Corporation shall be in the City of Washington, District of Columbia.

Third, that the objects and purposes of the Corporation shall be to buy or otherwise acquire reserves of crude petroleum from sources outside the United States, including the purchase or acquisition of stock in corporations owning such reserves or interests therein, and to store, transport, produce, process, manufacture, sell, market and otherwise dispose of such crude petroleum and the products derived therefrom; and the Corporation shall have the power and authority to do and perform all acts and things whatsoever necessary thereto, including, but without limitation, the power to borrow money and issue its secured or unsecured obligations therefor; to adopt and use a corporate seal; to make contracts; to sue and be sued; and to construct and operate outside the United States such refineries, pipe lines, storage tanks and other facilities as are necessary in connection with carrying out the objects and purposes of the Corporation as above stated.

Fourth, that the Corporation, including its franchise, its capital, reserves, surplus, income and assets shall be exempt from all taxation now or hereafter imposed by the United States, or any dependency or possession thereof, or by any state, county, municipality or local taxing authority except that any real property owned by the Corporation shall be subject to state, county, municipal or local taxation to the same extent according to its value as other real property is taxed.

Fifth, that the Corporation shall be an instrumentality of the United States Government, shall be entitled to the free use of the United States mails, and shall in all other respects be possessed of the privileges and immunities that are conferred upon the Reconstruction Finance Corporation under the Reconstruction Finance Corporation Act, as amended.

Sixth, that the total authorized capital stock of the Corporation shall be one million dollars ($1,000,000). Such stock shall be of one class, shall have a par value of $100 per share, and shall be issued for cash only.

Seventh, that the Corporation shall have existence until dissolved by Reconstruction Finance Corporation or by Act of Congress.

Eighth, that the stockholder shall not be liable for the debts, contracts, or engagements of the Corporation except to the extent of unpaid stock subscriptions.

Ninth, that the affairs and business of the Corporation shall be managed by a board of directors who shall be appointed by Reconstruction Finance Corporation pursuant to the provisions of this Charter and the By-Laws of the Corporation.

Tenth, that this charter and the By-Laws may be amended at any time by Reconstruction Finance Corporation.

In witness whereof, Reconstruction Finance Corporation has caused this Charter to be signed by its executive officer, Vice-Chairman of its Board of Directors, attested by its Secretary, and has caused its seal to be hereunto affixed this 30th day of June, 1943.

RECONSTRUCTION FINANCE CORPORATION,
by H. A. Mulligan, Vice-Chairman.

OUTLINE OF PROPOSED ARABIAN
PIPE-LINE AGREEMENT [1]

For brevity, Petroleum Reserves Corporation hereinafter is referred to as Government and the Arabian American Oil Co. and Gulf Exploration Co. are called the Companies.

Upon the recommendation of the War Department, Navy Department, Joint Chiefs of Staff and the Army and Navy Petroleum Board and with the approval of the Department of State, the aforementioned parties, in appreciation of the critical importance of reserves of petroleum in war and in peace and of the necessity of assuring to the military forces of the Nation and to the people of the United States adequate petroleum supplies, have agreed upon the principles of the understanding outlined below:

1. Government agrees to construct and to own and maintain a main trunk pipe-line system, including requisite facili-

1. *Congressional Record*, February 9, 1944, p. 1469.

ties, for the transportation of crude petroleum from a point near the presently discovered oil fields of Saudi Arabia and Kuwait to a port at the eastern end of the Mediterranean Sea. The size, capacity, location and terminal points of the pipe-line system shall be determined by Government. The gathering system for the delivery of oil to the intake terminus of the pipe-line shall be provided by the Companies. The Government shall determine the most feasible plan for the operation of the facilities and shall retain supervision thereof.

2. The Companies will cooperate with the various agencies of the United States Government in obtaining the necessary rights for the construction, maintenance, and operation of the pipe-line system and facilities.

3. The charges for pipe-line services shall include, in addition to current maintenance and operating costs, an amount sufficient to amortize within a period of 25 years the entire investment, together with interest and such net return to Government as may be agreed upon in the definitive contract. The parties shall agree upon an amount of oil to be tendered for transport by the companies as a minimum guaranteed amount in order that the Government will be guaranteed repayment of the items above specified, within the time limited. It is the intent that the companies will guarantee payment of the above items to the Government within the 25-year period.

4. Companies agree to perform at actual cost any work or services which the Government may request in connection with this project.

5. Government may make available to other oil producers or shippers the right to a portion of the capacity of the pipe-line system upon the agreement of such party or parties to assume pro rata the obligations undertaken by the companies, and upon such other terms and conditions as Government may specify, and also subject to the rights of the government of any country through which the pipe-line system passes.

6. Upon the following conditions the companies agree to maintain a crude oil petroleum reserve available for produc-

tion for the account of, and purchase by, the military forces of the United States:

(a) The reserve shall be 1,000,000,000 barrels of crude oil (gravity and specifications to be agreed upon) less amounts purchased by Government as provided for hereafter, or 20 per cent of the recoverable oil content of the companies' reserves if the total proved reserves be less than 5,000,000,000 barrels. The companies will use their best efforts to maintain the proved reserves above this amount.

(b) Government shall have the right (transferable to other governmental agency or agencies) to purchase for a period of 50 years for the military forces the 1,000,000,000 barrels of reserved crude oil, which the companies agree to deliver, if required by Government, at the rate of 30,000,000 barrels per year at times and quantities to be agreed upon. The aforesaid option is a continuing one and the Government is not required to purchase any crude oil during any particular period of time.

(c) Except in times of war or national emergency, if Government wishes to purchase more than 30,000,000 barrels during any calendar year, it must afford the companies reasonable notice to provide additional facilities required to meet such increased demand.

(d) Government shall have the option to purchase said quantity of reserved oil at a discount of 25 per cent below the market price in the Persian Gulf region for oil of like kind and gravity at the time and place of delivery, or at a discount of 25 per cent below the average of the market prices in the United States for oil of like kind and gravity, whichever of such prices is the lower at the time of delivery. The market price of crude oil in the United States shall be determined by the selection from time to time by the parties of certain points in the United States.

(e) The Government shall have the sole right to determine when and the manner in which the aforementioned reserve is drawn upon and may, if it elects, determine that said reserve has no relation to the purchase of petroleum made by the military forces from year to year in the normal course of supplying their requirements.

7. In times of war or other national emergency, Government shall have the first right and option, in addition to that specified in paragraph 6, to purchase all of the crude petroleum produced by the companies and all products thereof and shall pay therefor such price as the parties may agree upon at such time. Government shall specify what portion, if any, of such purchases constitutes withdrawals from the petroleum reserve provided in paragraph 6.

8. Prior notice of negotiations by companies with governments of any foreign countries relating in any manner to the sale of petroleum or products from their concessions in Saudi Arabia and Kuwait shall be given to the Department of State and to Government.

No sales of petroleum or products will be made by the companies to any government or the nationals of any government when, in the opinion of the Department of State, such sales would militate against the interests of the United States. Companies shall be afforded appropriate notice of such opinion.

The commercial and other policies and practices of the companies would conform to the foreign policy of the United States.

9. The agreement between the parties shall be sanctioned by the respective Governments of Saudi Arabia and Kuwait and nothing in this contract shall be construed to require action by the companies in violation of their covenants with said Governments under existing agreements. Companies agree to lend all possible assistance to Government in carrying out its obligations hereunder.

Companies will not construct or cause to be constructed any additional main pipe-line or pipe-lines for the westward transportation of crude petroleum or products from Saudi Arabia or Kuwait unless the capacity of contemplated pipe-line system installed by Government is insufficient to meet the requirements of the companies and, after reasonable notice from the companies, Government declines to install additional facilities. In any event, the companies agree at all times during the life of this agreement to utilize the pipe-line system contemplated herein to the fullest extent of its available capacity should their transportation requirements exceed the available capacity of the system.

10. This memorandum does not purport to contain a complete statement of the provisions of a contract to be entered into. It is a broad outline of certain of the essential provisions with the details and related provisions and other matters to be incorporated therein left for future determination.

11. In the execution and performance of this agreement, it is the desire and intention of the parties not only to promote and assist in the development of petroleum in the areas affected by this agreement, but also to promote the interests of the Governments of such areas, and to respect their sovereignty and protect their rights. It is the desire of the United States that American nationals that enjoy privileges with respect to petroleum in countries under foreign governments shall have an active concern for the peace and prosperity of such countries and shall exercise their rights with due regard to the rights, including that of political integrity, of the governments of such countries.

It is understood that the foregoing memorandum is subject to the approval of the board of directors of the parties and of their approval of a definitive contract containing all of the agreements of the parties. The foregoing is approved in principle, and I agree to recommend its approval to my board of directors.

        Harold L. Ickes, Petroleum Reserves Corporation.
        F. A. Davies, Arabian American Oil Co.
        J. F. Drake, Gulf Exploration Co.

The undersigned, presidents of Standard Oil Co. of California and the Texas Co., respectively, sole stockholders of the Arabian American Oil Co., are in accord with the foregoing in principle and agree to recommend its approval by their respective boards of directors and, subject to such approval, agree to recommend its approval by the board of directors of the Arabian American Oil Co.

> H. D. Collier.
> W. S. S. Rodgers.

The undersigned, president of the Gulf Oil Corporation, is in accord with the foregoing in principle and agrees to recommend its approval by the board of directors of the Gulf Oil Corporation, and subject to such approval, agrees to recommend its approval by the board of directors of the Gulf Exploration Co. Nothing herein shall require action in violation of existing contracts with the British Government or with any corporation in which the British Government has an ownership interest.

> J. F. Drake.

INDEX

Abadan, 28, 31, 42, 82, 181
Abqaiq, 60, 66
Aden, 48
American Independent Oil Company, 33, 98, 131
Anglo-American Oil Agreement, 95-100, 127, 185-90
Anglo-Egyptian Oil Fields, Ltd., 56
Anglo-Iranian Oil Company, 9, 21, 22, 26, 27, 39, 40-41, 43-44, 45, 181
Arabian-American Oil Company, concessions, 38, 55; employees, 62-63, 82; formation, 53; policies, 63, 80-83; production, 33, 60, 61

Bahrein Island, 2, 12, 27-28, 31, 48, 59, 61, 181
Bahrein Petroleum Company, 50, 58
Bain, J. S., 146, 155
Basing point system, 23, 140, 172

California Arabian Standard Oil Company, 52, 53, 59
California Texas Oil Company, 64
Caribbean, 15, 20, 140
Cartels, 9, 22, 45, 99, 102, 115, 175
Cie. Francaise des Petroles, 45, 55, 181
Colombia, 2
Committee of European Economic Cooperation, 25, 34, 35, 122-23

Concessions, 8, 37-57, 181; Arabia, 3, 13, 48-56, 131, 181; Egypt, 56; Iran, 40-43, 181; Iraq, 44-48, 181; other, 57
Conservation, 3, 16, 104, 142, 173-74

Dammam field, 59, 61, 74, 79, 82
D'Arcy, William, 40
De Golyer Report, 27, 51
Dhahran, 76, 82, 137

Eastern Gulf Oil Company, 49
Egypt, 27, 28, 56, 106
European Recovery Program, 34-35, 123, 139

France, 5, 10, 31, 44
Frankel, P. H., 22, 146, 167, 172
Feis, Herbert, 44, 91, 92
Foreign exchange, 35, 39, 41, 47, 67-69, 84, 138-39

Great Britain, 10, 12, 22, 41, 44, 47, 49, 95-100, 108, 136, 181, 185
Gulbenkian, C. S., 45, 181
Gulf Oil Company, 21, 49, 181

Hadramaut, 47
Haifa, 28, 30, 31, 48
Holman, Eugene, 140

Ibn Saud, 51, 72-73, 88-89
Ickes, Harold, 90-92, 190, 196
Imports, 22, 23. *See also* Petroleum and United States
International Cooperative Alliance, 104-5

199

International petroleum agreements, 95-100, 104, 116-22, 185, 192-96
International Trade Organization, 8, 9, 102, 121-22
Iran, 27, 28, 34, 40-43, 106
Iraq, 12, 26, 27, 34, 98, 106
Iraq Petroleum Company, 9, 28, 31, 44, 45-47, 55
Italy, 5

Jidda, 13, 54, 74

Kirkuk, 26, 30, 47-48
Kuwait, 2, 12, 27, 34, 48, 50-54, 98, 131, 181
Kuwait Oil Company, 66

Latin America, 3, 11, 170
Lebanon, 66, 106, 181
Loftus, John A., 11, 37, 100

Marshall Plan, 34, 35, 123, 129
Mexico, 2, 3, 21, 124
Middle East, oil reserves, 27, 28, 177, 181; political developments, 106-9; production, 15, 20, 23, 26-30, 177, 178, 181, 182, 183. See also Concessions
Middle East Pipeline Company, 66
Mosul, 28
Muscat, 47, 48

Near East Development Corporation, 45
Netherlands, 12, 13
Netherlands East Indies, 5, 13, 28

Oil industry. See Petroleum industry
Open door policy, 7, 10, 12

Palestine, 28, 57, 108, 129, 181
Persian Gulf, 11, 15, 20, 23, 24, 28, 29, 140-41, 171, 172
Petroleum, consumption, 32, 160, 161, 178, 183; costs, 5, 19, 20, 150, 152-54; demand, 16-20, 156-58, 160; discoveries, 29, 59, 60, 111, 181; exports, 179, 181; future trends, 24-25, 31-32, 183; geology, 14-16, 28, 29, 59; imports, 33, 179, 180; markets, 30-36, 64, 101, 127, 171; production, 2, 21, 34, 181; refining, 31, 35, 61, 137-38, 152-53, 169-70, 181; reserves, 2, 14-16, 21, 48, 177, 181; supply, 16-20, 32, 146, 156-57, 181; transportation, 34, 47-48, 101, 149-52, 181
Petroleum industry, capital intensity, 154-55; competition, 22, 98, 115, 158; economies of scale, 147-54; nationalization, 5, 7, 112-16; oligopoly control, 23, 102, 175; organization, 161-68
Petroleum Industry War Council, 94
Petroleum Reserves Corporation, 90-95, 190-96
Pipe lines, 30, 33, 34, 43, 47-48, 65-67, 129-30, 141, 149-51, 181, 184, 192-96
Price policy, 23, 24, 139-40
Profits, 69-70

Qatar, 27, 47, 48, 54, 98, 181

Ras Gharib, 56
Ras Tanura, 28, 61
"Redline Agreement," 9, 26, 45-46, 49
Reserves. See Petroleum
Revenue Act of 1932, 124
Riyadh, 72, 73
Riza Shah, 41, 106
Roumania, 21, 22

INDEX 201

Royal Dutch Shell Company, 13, 21, 22, 27, 45, 181
Royalties, 9, 57, 69-70, 83-84, 130, 131, 135, 181
Russia, 10, 15, 20, 22, 28, 42, 43, 177-78, 183

San Remo Conference, 12, 44
Saudi Arabia, agriculture, 73-75; education, 88-89; finance, 75-80, 84-88, 130; oil production, 27, 34; oil reserves, 27, 48-49; politics, 72-73, 81, 107, 108; religion, 73, 87
Sinclair Oil Company, 42, 98
Socony-Vacuum Oil Company, 21, 42, 181
Standard Oil Company of California, 21, 49, 51, 181
Standard Oil Company (New Jersey), 13, 21, 22, 43, 181
Subsidies, 20, 125
Synthetic fuels, 17-19
Syria, 28, 106, 129, 181

Tariffs, 5, 22, 31
Technological progress, 173-74
Texas Company, 21, 64-65, 181
Trans-Arabian Pipeline Company, 56, 65
Transjordan, 28, 57, 181
Tripoli (Lebanon), 48
Trucial Oman, 47-50, 181
Turkey, 44, 47, 107

United Nations, 100, 104
United States, diplomacy, 49, 51, 54; demand for oil, 16-20, 24, 111; export-import policy, 122-26, 130, 179, 180, 183; foreign investment, 4, 6, 7, 10, 35, 70, 137-38; Navy oil purchases, 24, 132-35; oil policy, 6, 7, 11-13, 44-45, 53-54, 81, 90-100, 112-16, 126-28, 168-70; oil reserves, 2, 15, 17, 21, 111

Venezuela, 2, 15, 20, 171

Yemen, 48, 99, 107

www.ingramcontent.com/pod-product-compliance
Lightning Source LLC
Chambersburg PA
CBHW021404290426
44108CB00010B/384